Artravesty
A Collection of Essays

by
Elena L. Rubinova

Pen and ink drawings by A.R. Welm

Alondra Press, LLC
www.alondrapress.com

Alondra Press Publishing, LLC
Houston, Texas 77072
lark@alondrapress.com

Library of Congress
Cataloguing-In-Publication # 2014954491

ISBN 978-0-9854909-4-2

This book may be purchased directly through
Alondra Press: *www.alondrapress.com*
email address: *lark@alondrapress.com*

Cover illustration, pen and ink drawings, and overall design
by A. R. Welm

With blk&wht reproductions of artwork from the Western
tradition.

Printed in the United States of America

To Sasha, of course.

Table of Contents

Author's Note   i

Introduction   v

On Second Commandment, Jews, and Abstract Art   1

By Aphrodite of Knidos: 13
A Personal Journey — From Goddess to Harlot

Mona Lisa vs. Modern American Womanhood   57

Nun vs. Venus   73

On Temptation: 81
Is he from Heaven or is he from Hell/
This deep-ingressing Gabriel?

Annunciation vs. Violation vs. Insemination   93

On Naughty Habits, Gods of Yore, and Kellogg Flakes   105

Intermezzo   123

The Black Madonna   131

The Golden Age   153

Ancient Mariners   179

Author's Note

François-Marie Arouet, better known by his *nom de plume*, Voltaire, once observed that it was easier for him to write books than to get them published; yet he kept scribbling. William Blake bemoaned a similar fate; yet he kept both writing poetry and drawing breathtaking pictures. In both cases, while the causes differed significantly, the effect was comparable.

When one finds oneself in such a stellar company *vis-à-vis* publishing, one is at once dwarfed and elated. Dwarfed more than elated, actually, because elation involves an uncomfortable degree of hubris—to the point where it borders on inadmissible. It is as if a comparison is encouraged between a speck of a desert sand and celestial beacons, which of course can never be entertained. Being dwarfed, on the other hand, is *very* admissible, indeed flattering, when dwarfed by geniuses. But suppose a miracle does happen, and one does get published—it is then very advisable to get up, straighten one's back, breathe deeply, and keep one's head on one's shoulders by thinking of all the books, the infinite number of books, that have been written, are presently being written, will be written—and published—and how many of them really matter? Very few. Obviously the Voltaires and Blakes of this world matter immensely, but compared to all the books *ever* written, how many Voltaires and Blakes are there? And yet there isn't a scribbler, I wager, but doesn't aspire not only to have his oeuvre published, but to have it widely read. Yet what chance is there that his composition will find its way in the swarm!

Even the successful books are often only successful for a season. Of course financial rewards of such a success are nothing to disdain, but one is never satisfied and always wants more. I suppose a writer of a popular book would, in addition to money, also like to be considered a *good* writer, and would be naturally disappointed if the recognition ended with that one volume. What about his other works? God knows how much time and effort the author had put into them, how much research he had undertaken, what anguish suffered on the road to publishing. And for what—to give some indifferent reader a few hours of recreation, or to distract him on a longish voyage? And then this reader forgets the book the moment it is read. But most authors don't even get that far.

The conclusion I have drawn from all this, is that the writer should derive his reward from the pleasure of writing, and from the topic of his inquiry, and try not to care too much about accolades or criticism, disappointment or triumph. Kipling's *If* comes uneasily to mind, which proposes a similar attitude on a wider scope, and on a wider scope this attitude, while admirable, is extremely difficult to achieve. But on a lesser scale, as I have learned, it *is* possible. My very talented artist of a daughter, who illustrated this book and who has a very rare ability to convey significant emotion through convincing and economic line, can spend hours drawing for her own pleasure, oblivious to everything else, including, alas, lucrative commissions. It is in the process of creation that she finds her reward, more so than in recognition, although, very human that she is, she is obviously not indifferent to praise.

It was also my daughter who insisted I put this book together out of various essays I had written as a result of conversations, discussions, questions brought up in class by my students, and other assorted stimuli. I never dreamt they would see the light of day, and wrote them for my own, and for my friends' amusement. They are not scholarly works; they are points of interest; and as such, are bestrewed with sacrilege that does not admit of foot-notes, some of it deliberate, some, unquestionably, due to ignorance. I suppose they may belong in the *belles-lettres* genre, which is, ultimately, all writing that does not fit into any major category such as fiction, drama, academic work etc. To have found Armando Benitez, the publisher of Alondra Press, who liked them well enough to agree to publish them as a book, has indeed been a miracle. Once he made the decision, he has been there for me through every step—reading, editing, correcting, advising—for which I am eternally grateful. The essays have been vastly re-thought and re-written from the originals. To have asked Barry Seldes, a true scholar and a genuine intellectual, to write an introduction to something he had to consider frivolous at best, superficial at worst, with little leeway in-between, was as cheeky as it was daunting. What he has written, I must humbly express, is as gratifying as it is unmerited.

ELR

Introduction

by Barry Seldes

Here is a delightful, short but far-ranging set of commentaries on some chief foibles of Western culture, written by a brilliant stylist, with excellent sketches by A.R. Welm.

Imagine yourself at a discussion of the eternal feminine in all her erotic powers, its leader (our author, Ms. Rubinova), a Diotima of Mantineia, with unsurpassed wisdom concerning love and beauty, who also happens to be a learned professor of the history of Western art, moreover, armed with rapier wit. The targets of that wit? All manner of pettifoggery, foible and outright cynicism that have surrounded and sought to distort, hide or deny the eternal feminine erotic. You will find our Diotoma discoursing on paintings and sculptures, and the manners and mores represented by them, in terms that can be simultaneously ravishing and reverent, sensitive and iconoclastic. Pay attention as you read: there are enough double entendres to keep you rollicking in laughter as you are taken on an exquisite romp through great swaths of Western cultural iconography.

To begin with, this commentary on our culture contains any number of surprises, not least Ms. Rubinova's startling connection between Biblical prohibitions of certain graven images, and early 20th century Soviet *avant garde* abstraction (which latter, by the way, stands in for one of our author's bêtes noirs: non-representational art). Our author has Praxiteles' *Aphrodite of Knidos* come alive to describe her voluptuous form in the language of a self-connoisseur, and then to be reborn as Botticelli's *Venus*, with fascinating contrasts and comparisons made possible by reproductions and by Welm's outstanding artwork. But I remind that it is not art history as such, but a history of the manners and mores, and artistic representations of and about the feminine. But be warned: our author is not a modern or postmodern feminist. Hers is a classicist's feminism that would preserve the values of a Diotima that honor feminine grace and noble charm, values under assault in today's culture. Thus Ms. Rubinova's suggestion that the passage from Leonardo's *Mona Lisa* and Giorgione's *Sleeping Venus* to Picasso's *Les Demoiselles d'Avignon* and to de Kooning's *Woman* is a passage insensibility from a Renaissance cultivation of depth, to a modern cultivation of surface. Or in other words, from the mind as signified by *La Gioconda's* visage, to so many vacuous facial contortions and distortions that, to our author, express the ever dissatisfied narcissism of our contemporary culture.

Now, Ms. Rubinova will not allow herself to fall into depression over what she regards as a dreadful collapse in taste, for in short order she returns to her great theme on Aphrodite and her descendants with a discourse on "*Nun Versus Aphrodite*, " exemplifying her great exploration of the eternal erotic within the eternal feminine. But, strangely enough, she conjures up, of all things, Botero's *Nun Eating an Apple!*—a cute and sexless nun who seems poles apart from Diotima's goddess. But then the revelation: for in the privacy of her room, the rather piggish little nun has removed her habit to reveal her real self as .... an Aphrodite! She is Botero's *Venus*, nude, corporeal all right, but in the sense of generously endowed, very sumptuous, not otherworldly *à la* Giorgione, but quite of this world. Of course she will soon have to re-habit herself to comply with command, but the secret is out. Women, be they Aphrodite or the cloistered nun, are erotic beings, even, (especially?) in the cloister. For centuries, nuns forced into celibacy were ruthlessly confronted by paintings and sculptures of so many Catherines of Sienna and other saintly sufferers pierced by sword and arrows in their erotic parts—representations of the very forbidden acts that were no doubt deciphered by nuns who lived within their rich fantasy lives. In fact, speaking of fantasy lives, Catherine of Sienna wore what she swore to be Christ's foreskin as her (invisible but to herself) wedding band! And speaking of foreskins and divine purpose .... well, let's just say that Ms. Rubinova will not let **that** topic go quietly into the night: reporting, in a succeeding discourse, that the rib that supposedly figured in Eve's creation was no rib; it was the more usual appendage, but it got lost in translation.

There are many other moments of truth-telling iconoclasm on these pages. A major example of patriarchal hypocrisy is the Reims Cathedral sculpture of *The Annunciation*, the angel Gabriel leering at 14-year-old Mary as his hand gestures toward that what he's got in store for her. One of the best moments in the text is the brilliantly told report that the Biblical creation story was following something like a cookbook recipe that was already (first?) laid down long before by Egyptians. And then there is Ms.

Rubinova's short treatise on attempts by Christian religious and American breakfast cereal magnates to curb masturbation. As for the double entendres, no better examples can be found than in her disquisition on the rise of the British public schools. I told you this book is far-ranging!

October, 2014

On Second Commandment, Jews, and Abstract Art

There will not be much discussion of abstract art in this volume, although some modern art will be considered. But as abstract art is very much part of our lives, and certainly a very large part of our museums, I've decided to get it done and over with by beginning this volume with this piece, which considers possible origins of conceptual art. There have been multiple studies on the subject of course, and perhaps the thesis I am about to propose has been advanced before. I hear that everything has been advanced before. But as I am unaware of it, I make bold to introduce it here with appropriate apologies to my possible precursor. I have no doubt that many a connoisseur will find this thesis objectionable, in which case I should warmly welcome a debate, for although I am far less hopeful than Socrates was of truth prevailing through polemic, I also humbly submit to his far greater and far more ancient wisdom.

Before the likes of Helen Frankenthaller and Yves Klein, there were the likes of Mark Rothko and Jackson Pollock, and before them there were the Russian Suprematists, and before them there was the Second Commandment:

"Thou shalt not make to thyself an idol, nor likeness of anything, whatever things are in the heaven above, and whatever are in the earth beneath, and whatever are in the waters under the earth. Thou shalt not bow down thyself to them, nor serve them; for I the Lord thy God am a jealous God, visiting the iniquity of the fathers upon the children unto the third and fourth generation of them that hate me..." (Exodus 20:4-5).

As everyone knows, there were ten key injunctions that Moses received from Jehovah on Mount Sinai, inscribed with God's own forefinger upon two stone tablets. It is the second of the ten injunctions that concerns us here. Of the stone tablets there were two sets, the original and the copy. The original was smashed to pieces by Moses in wild frenzy, when, on coming down from the mountain forty days after he had gone up, almost out of breath what with his extremely heavy burden, he saw his people doing exactly the opposite of what Jehovah had inscribed, with his own forefinger, upon two stone tablets. The poor homeless emigrants, unaware yet of any tablets, or of any commandments, having despaired of seeing their fearless leader ever again (what with his unexpectedly long absence), and utterly lost in the wilderness with no guidance whatever, had turned to their traditional tribal beliefs. They cast a sculpture of a Golden Calf, which they placed upon a make-shift altar, to which they sacrificed, and around which they danced in confused hysteria of hope. Indeed, to make this effigy, they stripped their women of all their gold jewelry (objections notwithstanding), melted it down, and recast it into the worshipful bovine. And lo and behold! – the Calf obliged, and sent them back their chief - unharmed, and with a couple of

4

stone steles under his arms with something presumably useful written on them.

Imagine their shock when they saw the aforementioned chief go into a hissy fit, foam at the mouth, smash the two tablets, divine finger and all, and with no explanation, order his faithful henchmen, the Levites, to go "each of you kill his brother, his friend, his neighbor." The obliging Levites, who had merrily danced around the Bull and sacrificed along with everyone else just minutes before Moses showed up, quickly weighed their options and having clearly decided that Moses and his god ruled the day, and that their own hide needed saving, presently "obeyed and about three thousand of the people died that day." Moses was pleased with the results: "Today you have consecrated yourselves to the Lord completely," he spoke to his tired assistants while they were wiping their relatives' blood off their hands and knives, "because you have turned each against his own son and his own brother and so have this day brought a blessing upon yourselves." (Exodus 32: 27-28).

The golden calf was accordingly demoted to the lower case and sent packing— broken down, pulverized with Jehovah's help, and mixed with the sand. The women, who had lost their husbands, their sons, and their brothers, no longer worried about their lost jewelry. Their valiant leader, meanwhile, hiked back up Mount Sinai to procure that second set of the two stone steles—the copy of the first. He needed it, for he did, after all, feel obliged to give his people some explanation as to why he had half the tribe slaughtered, if he were to command their obedience for the next two-score years. Trying to clarify it in his own words, stuttering all the while (he had that inconvenient defect from birth, as attested by the Scriptures), may not have won him much popularity in the end. This second round trip took another forty days, but this time what was left of the tribe did not budge, but patiently waited for him to return with the promised written account and instructions.

When he finally did return for good, he showed them the refashioned tablets with the Ten Commandments chiseled upon them. The greater part of these was essentially the stuff that other gods bid their people to do or not to do, in oral or written form, whether the people be Egyptians, Babylonians, Hittites, Amorites, or any other nation Hebrews had come into contact with. It was about keeping religious holidays, respecting one's parents, not stealing, not lying, not wenching, not murdering, etc. Everyone knew those, at least in theory, but not everyone followed them to the letter. To be sure, their own commander had just murdered three thousand men.

The two *very* different instructions were the one about the peerless god to the exclusion of all others, and the other, which was an extension of the first, about the prohibition of any representation— "... nor likeness of anything, whatever things are in the heaven above, and whatever are in the earth beneath, and whatever are in the waters under the earth (sic)." This god evidently construed all imagery produced by man's hands as idolatry - an intolerable competition to his own greatness. To the people steeped in centuries of tribal polytheism, the First Commandment had to appear oddly intolerant, and the Second simply incomprehensible, for how was one to worship anything invisible?!

Indeed, this bedraggled lot of Hebrews must have been greatly puzzled by all this. No other people did anything of the sort. Egyptians, for instance, who were a much more ancient race, had a beautiful country of their own, given to them by their many generous gods, whom these Egyptians thanked in continuous worship, with no one telling them they couldn't venerate whom they liked, or couldn't paint them, or sculpt them in all their divine metamorphoses. To be sure, they even had a living god. "Pharaoh" they called him, and even he didn't forbid worship of other gods, whereas this Moses wasn't even divine, and yet was bidding them to ban all gods except the one of the stone stele. He couldn't even prove that the Commandments were written by the divine finger anymore. Even if the first set was so inscribed, it was destroyed, and surely no respectful deity makes *a copy* himself...

But they dared not complain, because the Second Commandment had a further stipulation concerning man-made imagery, should anyone disobey and make it anyway— "... Thou shalt not bow down to them, nor serve them; for I the Lord thy God and a jealous God, visiting the iniquity of the fathers upon the children, unto the third and fourth generation of them that hate me..." And then, in the Third Commandment, there was the bit about "... the Lord will not leave unpunished the man who misuses his name." And later on "... a day will come when I shall punish them for their sins." (Exodus 32:34-35), etc., etc. And of course there were three thousand dead, murdered in broad daylight, right here at the foot of Mount Sinai, many still unburied and beginning to reek, which made the Commandments' threats very real indeed.

The Jews obeyed. In their subsequent thrice-millenarian history they would breach, individually or collectively, to a greater or lesser degree, just about every one of the commandments—except the first two. They would worship the one and only god, and until the advent of the twentieth century broke all boundaries, they would never draw, paint, or sculpt any of their God's creation, let alone himself. And not only Jews did it (or rather didn't do it), but the early adherents of Christianity and then Islam—the other two monotheistic religions rooted in Judaism— did the same, Islam holding out longer than Christianity.

Christianity couldn't do without imagery for long, and soon found a way around the prohibition by explaining to God the Father, to the Son, and to the Holy Ghost (as well as to themselves) that there must be pictures for those who can't read—pictures that clarified Biblical stories, and that these pictures were not worshipful in themselves, but only representing worshipful ideas that needed to be explained through illustration. Thank heaven they did it—we'd have no Michelangelo or Raphael without this excuse. And yet, over time, many a self-appointed religious reformer, in his anxiety to purify whatever clerical practices he deemed objectionable, was presently condemning the Church's breaking of the Second Commandment. Witness Luther and Calvin, and the destruction, by their followers, of paintings, statuary, stained glass windows—in short, denuding all places of worship they got their hands on. So much the worse for us, because some of the most astonishing art of Northern Renaissance was destroyed in the process. But the Second Commandment was fulfilled, and God, Luther and Calvin were pleased.

Still, what artists learned from Renaissance onward could not be undone—for they learned to represent god's creation as it had never been seen before. Indeed, they themselves became grand creators of natural appearances, often on par with the Creator Himself.

But let us fast-forward across time to the aforementioned advent of the twentieth century. By now the Impressionists had cancelled out "the form" which Renaissance artists had discovered and bequeathed to later generations of artists, and the Expressionists had erased all appearances of conventional decorum in art. There had been Symbolism and Surrealism, with Munch baring his soul as a representative of the former, and Dali making a mockery of his as a representative of the latter. And there had also been Fauvism and Cubism, which Matisse and Picasso used respectively to compete with each other in their *épater le bourgeois* rivalry, with Picasso the ultimate champion. And there had been no end of other "isms" besides.

Meantime history was taking its toll. Over a hundred years earlier there was the French Revolution, which showed that God wasn't necessary for one's happiness and fulfillment, and then there was Nietzsche who proclaimed God to be dead altogether. Not dead in the literal sense, of course. Not like those three thousand Hebrews that He made Moses slaughter with the Levites' help three millennia earlier, but dead in an ethical sense—no longer a practicable basis for any absolute moral principle. And soon enough there was the first stage of the Russian revolution (Russians did everything the French did, but even more murderously), the bourgeois one that allowed Russian Jews to leave their shtetls and settle in big cities, and also to enroll in universities and—miracle of miracles—in art academies. The second stage, Reign of Terror, was soon to follow, when Russians decided to be original and innovative, and had it last seventy years, whereas the French only had their Reign of Terror for less than a miserly year. But that's another story and we must return to the Jews. At least those who survived unremitting butchery, and/or left the country.

Since time immemorial Jews were forbidden to represent anything that *breathed,* or even *looked* as if it might breathe, for fear it might be construed as idolatry. For the Second Commandment could be interpreted differently—from disallowing sculpture only, or sculpture and painting, or even a diminutive drawing so long as it represented nature. Ultimately, the safest thing was not to touch a brush or a chisel, or a pencil at all, and they didn't. But now that God was dead, and the Revolution cancelled out all boundaries, traditions, and prohibitions, they were *free* to do as they liked, unbounded by ritual. Consequently they ran amok, as was only to be expected - the forbidden fruit syndrome. But however drunk they were with this newly found license, they were still Jewish; still the people of The

Book; and the Ten Commandments, however much they may scorn them, psychologically were still The Law. It must have been completely titillating, exhilarating, and invigorating for the likes of Malevich, Pevzner, Delaunay, Lissitzky to trample primordial tradition—ostensibly—once it was allowed; but surely it couldn't have been so easy inwardly. The millenarian prohibition on depicting 'likenesses' had to have sunk very deeply into their soul.

Which is where western Europeans, with their "isms" experiments came very handy. With this bit between their teeth, and the strong wind of giddy emancipation in their mane, Malevich & Co. galloped through the gates thrown wide-open for them by their western precursors—the gates through which these precursors had not quite dared go themselves—into pure abstraction. Reason they didn't dare was probably that, unlike the Jews, Christians did have the tradition of depicting natural appearances engrained in their soul. Throughout the late nineteenth and early twentieth century, they had done an exemplary job of twisting and distorting these appearances, by pen, brush and chisel, into near-unrecognizable shapes, but pure abstraction was another thing altogether—still an uncharted territory. But they did not mind so much if someone else went exploring. They had produced enough outrage after all, and could now sit on their laurels and let others put their best brush avant-guard. And the Jewish artists obliged. Pure abstraction was safe; it was non-representational; it didn't *breathe.* A bevy of impressive terminology could be (and was) summoned to serve it: Rayonism, Suprematism, Constructivism, Cubo-Futurism ... And when it came to moral, esthetic and ethical rationalizations, justifications, and higher purposes that were needed to explain this new trend so those who might wish to follow could feel elevated rather than bewildered—that was easy enough.

After all, were they not evoking the transcendentally mystical, non-representational, un-perceivable nature of the Creator—incomprehensible to mere mortals, and only intelligible to the CHOSEN?

By Aphrodite of Knidos: A Personal Journey — From Goddess to Harlot

"Beauty is truth, truth beauty—that is all / Ye know on earth, and all ye need to know." Immortal Keats speaking of immortal Aphrodite's world.

After the rigors of the previous article, it is only appropriate to revert to the world of beauty, for beauty leads us to God. It is also befitting to revert to the world of art denied to the protagonists of the first article by their stern creator and His Second Commandment. This one is written in the voice of Aphrodite of Knidos, the most famous sculpture of antiquity, and is the longest piece in this volume, which makes sense considering our goddess's long and arduous journey from her world to ours.

▼

Once upon a time, on the island of Knidos, one Praxiteles, brandishing a chisel, cut me out of Parian marble, and so beautiful he sculpted me, so alluring and irresistible, that the islanders issued forth a universal sigh of wonder and placed me in a lovely circular shrine for all to see, calling me Aphrodite, whom no one could see, and, as Aphrodite of Knidos, my fame spread throughout the world.

It was only natural that Praxiteles fell in love with me (as all men did), but unlike another sculptor, Pygmalion by name, he could not convince my divine namesake to turn me into flesh and blood, and a good thing too, for, in marble, I had mastery over him, whereas the opposite would be true

15

were I alive, and I shouldn't have liked it. Besides, I lived much longer in marble than I would have done in flesh and blood. And, in marble, I was never forgotten, whereas I certainly would have been in flesh and blood. And furthermore, if anyone hungers after the truth, which one rarely does, I can tell him/her that this Pygmalion never lived, let alone carved; his legend originated after *my* Praxiteles sculpted *me*, and, as I may have modestly mentioned above, my marble self was so lifelike, so soft, delicate and desirable, translucent and sensuous, that men were tempted to do (and did) tremendously naughty things in my presence, at night, having caused themselves to be locked up alone with me in my small shrine (where there was barely enough room for *me*), with only the full moon for a witness, after giving up their life's savings, in bribe, to the shrine's overseer for the privilege. But I suppose boys *will* be boys. At any age, under all moons, and in all times.

You must know, honorable Reader, that at this time, in ancient Greece, whether the moon was full or otherwise, beauty that aroused physical passion, be it of marble or of flesh, was given religious status. And nowhere was it more so than in Knidos, an island off the south coast of Asia Minor, upon whose verdant outcroppings my divine namesake arrived sailing on a large shell, after being born from fertilization of diaphanous sea foam by the mutilated penis of Uranus. Reader, don't flinch—Uranus, wide and starlit, was known for child abuse, to the great grief of Gaea, his long-suffering spouse, with the consequence that she finally felt enough was enough and convinced her last-born, Cronus, fully grown and able despite abuse, to arm himself with a sharp metal sickle for the purpose of slashing off his cruel

16

father's procreative organ. Cronus, who was in love with his mother, although he didn't know of Herr Freud at the time, was only too ready to oblige, and it was as the result of this surgical procedure, and of consequent penetrating, by his sire's amputated organ, of the sea into which it fell, that the goddess of love was born. Unaccountably, once the son assumed power, after getting rid of his impotent father, he was as rotten to his own children, whom he had the habit of swallowing live, as his father had been to his, for which he too suffered consequences, but I am diverting (as I am prone to do), and must return to the most important subject—*me.*

The fact that my divine namesake, once born in this unconventional fashion, landed in Knidos and no other island, was emphatically asserted by the Knidians, even though other islands did beg to differ. The fact that I, personally, lived on Knidos, is uncontestable. There is a story in Pliny the Elder (one of my admirers and Admiral of the Roman fleet, who unhappily died during the eruption of Vesuvius), that Praxiteles originally carved me for a different island—perhaps one of those that begged to differ. But that foolhardy and quarrelsome island, according to Pliny, misguidedly believed that true beauty could never be nude, and rejected me (unfathomable!), thus affording the Knidians the chance to profit by their rivals' provincial prudery, and become possessors of the most beautiful and famous statue in antiquity, if I may say so myself.

Still another ancient author has left a vivid account of a visit to my sanctuary, and although I don't remember his particular aspect, or his name, for there were so many visitors, I acknowledge deep gratitude to this literary pilgrim for his chronicler's pains. He writes, perfectly correctly, that instead of a usual paved courtyard, with which other, inferior sculptures may have been surrounded in their respective sites, mine was encircled by the most exquisite fruit trees, among which hung vines heavily weighted down with festoons of succulent grapes. In the midst of all this fertile abundance, fertility being perfectly agreeable to me and to my divine namesake, was a small shrine. An overseer would open its front door to afford anxious pilgrims a furtive glimpse at me, white and radiant in contrast to surrounding verdure. For a price, the glimpse could be prolonged. I didn't mind; nor did my divine namesake. I was carved in the moment of presently stepping into a ritual bath (it would be called 'candid camera' millennia later), with my left hand still holding the shift I had just slowly drawn from my shoulders. The gesture of my right hand, half hiding, half revealing my nether region, drew all eyes to this source of my powers by my very attempt at inadequate concealment. Praxiteles caused my lips to part in a soft smile in anticipation of the gentle water's gentle touch, and although I had certainly not laid aside the majesty of the Olympian (nor could I), in my sculptor's adroit hands I was as a living woman of stunning beauty, ready to receive, ready to respond. All who saw me, felt that the instincts they shared with beasts they also shared with gods. So overwhelmed was my literary pilgrim, and so generous to the overseer, that when all lesser mortals were gone, the overseer opened the back door of the shrine for the author to admire this aspect of me as well, and the author writes most exquisitely that his enthusiasm redoubled.

About two hundred years after these events, the Romans came to my beloved country, bearing a sword. They came, they saw, and they were conquered. The conquerors, says their poet Horace (another one of my admirers), were led captive by the conquered. Just at the time when Rome triumphed over all lands, defeated Greece swayed over the Roman mind. Just at the time when Greece lost its political scepter, the empire of her language and of her arts became universal through Roman reverence. Heretofore, frugal in puritan simplicity, Rome was ignorant of refinement. Thereafter, she succumbed to the cult of beauty—the cult of Aphrodite. Endless copies were made of me in Greece for Roman aristocracy; endless copies of copies were mechanically made in Rome for lesser consumption.

Reader, I shall now hopscotch through two thousand disagreeable years. It may take me a longish paragraph, but considering that in that space I must account for two millennia, please bear with me, for I must explain the inexplicable as economically as I can.

Ares, called Mars by the Romans, the father of Romulus and Remus and the bellicose lover of my divine namesake, sitting in his Temple of Mars Ultor in the Forum of Augustus, could talk of Rome till the end of times, roaring with gleeful laughter while brandishing his shield and wielding his heavy sword. But I have fewer words than Ares on the subject. Rome did not create beauty. She copied it. The victory of the foreign taste over her was as decisive, as it was enduring and unrivaled. The Divine Feminine was lost in the copying. About fifty full-size Roman replicas of me had survived the intervening centuries, buried deep in the soil of the lost civilization, but by the look of them, once dug up, male observers of these facsimiles must have found it easy to abstain from not only tremendous naughtiness in their presence, but even the modest naughtiness. The Romans called me Venus, instead of Aphrodite, and Venus was a different creature, no longer unique, but a subordinate one, a copy of the original. But at least Rome tried. She could never love as Greece loved; she lacked the delicacy of feeling, the subtlety of the mind, the competence of the hand; but she tried to the best of her ability, and, imperfect philosopher that I am, I was satisfied. For one cannot expect a recently civilized race to give more than it can. Credit goes to it for the effort. The original, meanwhile, was lost. The goddess, my divine namesake, must have sunk back into the wine-dark sea, whence she had come centuries earlier, the product of that unmentionable mating that I mentioned above.

It was the Christian centuries, which followed the fall of Rome, that spelled my doom. Love was outlawed, laughter forbidden, *joie de vivre* proscribed, physical beauty demonized. Why should anyone do it to themselves, I can't imagine. This new creed, a hodge-podge of multiple eastern cults, worshipping the cross when crucifixion was no longer practiced, and venerating the ethereal at the expense of the real, had obliterated the most natural and tender feeling in existence, earthly love. Sleeping Beauty may have lay somnolent, on a bed of roses surrounded by briar, for a hundred years. I lay in a coma, despised and forgotten, for a millennium.

The unlikely prince who awoke me was one Sandro Botticelli. An eccentric man he was, who dreamed wonderful dreams, and in one of them he saw Aphrodite freshly emerged from the sea foam, on her shell again, being blown by the eager winds toward Knidos... or Cyprus... or was it Florence now, where Botticelli painted his dreams into reality? I was changed in this dream of his, and also in his consequent painting. Of course I was changed!—a millenarian slumber could not be ignored. I was not quite sure of my bearing, not quite understanding what was happening to me. I *was* ethereal. Was I still slumbering? But the same slumber had also kept me eternally young—soft and supple—delicate and desirable—translucent and tempting. Instead of a shift, my left hand now held a twist of my long cascading blond hair with which it also concealed the aforesaid source of my power. The right hand now half hid, half covered, my breasts. It did not cover enough of course, and the aspect of said breasts was one of the most satisfying the eye could rest upon. How happy I am that it was Botticelli's eye!

Reader, I must divulge a secret to you as to how this came about; a great mystery of which you, of course, were completely unaware. Aphrodite never died; she is an immortal goddess—she cannot die. She lived deep in the hearts of men, transcendent in her beauty, ubiquitous in her presence, eternally patient in her intent. It was she who sent the dream to Botticelli. She knew he was ready. She knew that after endless centuries of rejection, the world was ready to receive her (and me) again. Her awakening had been bespoken. A homesickness for classical antiquity fell upon the Italian world about this time, and for the deeply cultured circle of my treasured Lorenzo de Medici, this nostalgia was wrought with poetry, with beauty, and with love. Through Horace, Virgil, and Lucretius, who had all written exquisitely about my world, and whose poetry had been recovered and admired in the Medici world, a man of Renaissance could glimpse it tantalizingly. Angelo Poliziano, the poet, and my treasured Lorenzo's cherished friend, could recover it faintly in Greek and Latin, or more rarely, in Italian verse.

But the Italian loves to see, and here was the difficulty, for the fertile soil of Florence was meager in yielding up the likes of me and my lot—the old marbles, visual manifestations of the distant and dreamy past. Yet fortune comes to the blessed, and before Botticelli painted me, he was summoned to Rome to work on the frescoes in the old Pope Sixtus's new Chapel. Antiques, which back in Florence were confined to just a few collections, lay all around him. No groundwork could be undertaken, no field freshly dug, without at least some fragments of my world coming to light, and often the whole sculptures were uncovered. From the thickets and vineyards of the Palatine, our nude figures emerged without shame or comment, and dear Botticelli took notice. Having trembled with unfulfilled aspirations and breathed exquisite nostalgias that imbued the very souls of the humanists of Lorenzo's Platonic Academy with its cult of Beauty, Botticelli could envision the visual ingredients of the dream that my divine namesake had sent him, and with the help of the Roman marbles, he was ready. It could never be like the original to be sure, but dreams dreamt by a Botticelli, produce bewitching imagery.

Back in Florence, when an obliging member of the Medici family asked him to recreate *Aphrodite Anadyomene,* he was warmly enthusiastic. This obliging Medician had just read the recently recovered writings of the unfortunate Pliny the Elder who had perished in Pompeii, in which Pliny described the *Anadyomene* as painted about the same time my Praxiteles carved me, by Praxiteles's contemporary, Apelles by name, whom I knew of course, for he was as famous a painter as my Praxiteles was a sculptor. He used me as a model for the *Anadyomene,* since he felt no living woman

could compare to me in beauty, form or grace, on which point he was of course accurate. Apelles painted his version of me not about to step into a bath, as my Praxiteles had done, but having just risen from the waves (hence *Anadyomene*) and drifting toward the shore on a large seashell. It was a glorious picture, admired by the great Alexander himself, and I admired it too—it was like looking in a mirror and seeing a goddess. I remember it vividly, but, unlike Praxiteles's version of me, no copy of Apelles's *Anadyomene* survived, thus compelling the Medician to ask that Botticelli reproduce Apelles's painting based on literary descriptions, as well as on my marble copies. The lucky Medician received *The Birth of Venus* – Prince Botticelli's awakening kiss upon Apelles's millenarian Aphrodite.

Reader, unlike me, you shall never know what the Apelles's original looked like, but as Botticelli's picture still exists, you know what *it* looks like, and I must tell you how pleased I am with his creation. Two thousand years is a long time to slumber, and I alone know how one feels on awakening. Well, I and this young Florentine, who miraculously understood my mood of hesitation and reserve, and thus rendered me still in a reverie, looking ahead, yet not seeing. I look wistful and melancholy, which I did not do in the Apelles version, when I had no reason for this frame of mind. My proportions are properly classical, but my stance is not, which is only natural, considering I was laying down for so long, and am still unsteady on my feet. Therefore, unlike the Apelles's version, I am not so much standing but floating. I may as well be still lying down, with my lovely hair tussled on celestial pillows (very Renaissance is my hair; those men knew a gorgeous apparition when they saw one—whether in life or in dream). Because my left foot makes no pretence at supporting my body, it is a good thing I *am* floating, for Botticelli made my position in the shell so precarious, were I to press down my weight, as light and slender as I am, the shell would turn over, alas, and I would tumble back into the waves most indecorously, which is unacceptable for any female with elegant pretentions, but *most* unacceptable for an Olympian. Mercifully, there is no fear of that, as I float toward the shore, glimpsing unfulfilled desires in the eternally deferred goal of earthly love. Hence my melancholy. I obey my destiny with resignation and dreamy modesty - almost contrite at the confusion I am fated to produce among mortals. My introversion here has little to do with the whole-souled sensuousness of Apelles's (or Praxiteles's) classical version. It has much to do, however, with the divine and earthly love that Florentine Neo-Platonists spent so many delectable hours trying to balance, eagerly practicing the earthly version, while worshiping the divine. And they were recondite in both.

It will take another artist to shake Sleeping Beauty fully out of her trance and to reintroduce her into the world of reality. It will take Raphael, that enthusiastic womanizer (Botticelli's tastes lay elsewhere), to succeed at this ambitious task. Unkind gossip has it that Raphael died at age 37 from over-exhaustion after a night of over-indulging, and I love unkind gossip as much as the next goddess, always encouraging, at the feasts of the gods, those to sit next to me who have something wicked to say about anyone else. But this is not the time or place for this penchant of mine. What I truly wish to emphasize, at the risk of sounding stuffy and academic, which is a narrator's worst nightmare, is Raphael's innate and uncanny gift of sensual perception, and if he chose to practice this gift in his carnal occupations as well as in his artistic aspirations, who am I, the goddess of love, to point a finger. If only he lived longer. But one conducts one's life as one is able (one's character is one's destiny, as the saying goes), and we all know the futility of beguiling conditionals. Let us be grateful for what we have. This man, in his thirty-seven years, spanned the lifetimes and achievements of multiple nonagenarians and influenced all consequent generations of artists. And of all his marvelous talents, the talent which was most completely his own, and seems to have come from the radiant center of his joyous personality, was his power of grasping the ideal through the senses, and bringing it to life. Glory of glories!—in the beautiful villa Farnesina, on the verdant western bank of the Tiber, he brought antiquity to life.

Let me tell you, Reader, about this sublime art-filled house, whose paintings, frescoes, and sculptures still fill its halls, all existing in heavenly harmony, never having been stripped or removed from the home for which they were meant, to fill, in orphan-like sadness, indifferent spaces of passionless museums.

The Farnesina (named after a later owner) was built in the "countryside" by Agostino Chigi, the richest man in Christendom in the first half of the sixteenth century, on his doctor's orders to curb his lust for filthy lucre (personally, I see nothing wrong in this particular addiction), and to relax his overwrought nerves. In those days, the "countryside" was everything that surrounded Rome's miniscule center, which had shrunk considerably since the days of the emperors. It included land along the western bank of the Tiber, where, in the days of those emperors, patrician Romans built their vacation homes. Cicero wrote about wanting to buy a villa in this area (he never did; he was too busy talking). Catullus's infamous lover, Clodia, owned property in these parts and received better looking suitors than Catullus, driving Catullus mad. Also driving him to write glorious poetry that Caesar loved (and I did too). But back to the Tiber's western bank. Even Emperor Augustus' daughter Julia, when in Rome during long summer afternoons, would enjoy the breeze that wafted up from the luxuriant river. That was before she was exiled to a desert island for consorting with half the Roman aristocracy and their slaves. The male half. As you see, the area had an irresistible aura of sensuousness and transgression.

Agostino hired a famous architect to design his villa in the style of Emperor Nero's Golden House, which at this time had just been unearthed. Our banker's embrace of this imperial den of iniquity would revolutionize architectural trends in summer homes and palaces for the next two centuries. He had pagan themes revived in audacious full-scale frescoes. On the walls of the Farnesina, we, the gods and the goddesses, frolicked, and upon the ceiling of the Great Loggia, my dear boy, Eros (who finally got caught up in his own net of mischief), and Psyche (the boy could have done much better in my opinion) were pledging marriage vows before the entire Olympian assembly. I did advise him to wait and see how things went on, sort of wet one's feet before the plunge, but he wouldn't listen ... and plunged. And even made Psyche immortal, this insignificant earthling.

Mythology was reborn in high style in the gardens as well, where ancient statuary lined flower-strewn walkways, while an impromptu theater was set up for viewing plays by ancient comedians. The villa became a hymn to the goddess of LOVE—a hymn to ME. My boy's marriage was chosen as the main theme because Agostino himself wished to be married soon, to the most beautiful creature in existence, and

27

looking forward to the triumph of physical union with corporeal beauty more voluptuous than anything the revival of paganism had yet achieved, he wished to have the most extraordinary artist for his lust, as well as for his money; he wished to have Raphael. Raphael, however, although Agostino's close friend, had papal orders to fulfill, and as we all know, both on earth and on Mt. Olympus, friendship is friendship, but business is business, and a Pope's commissions come before a banker's. While Raphael did agree to work on his friend's love house, and did most of the designs, they were executed by his pupils. Except one.

Farnesina is glorious, yet by far the best work there, and the only one entirely by Raphael's hand, is *Galatea*—the *Knidian* in action. I dare say that probably nothing in painting gives a more convincing idea of the lost masterpieces of antiquity.

Whatever they've called me and those like me through the ages—Aphrodite, Venus, Galatea, or any other classical beauty, the harmony by which Raphael gave perfection to the female form was never, for him, the product of calculation or conscious refinement. You can trust me in that, for in my present excitement, I am turning into an art historian, with the best knowledge and appreciation of them all, by virtue of my superior hierarchical standing. Others, like Leonardo or Michelangelo, wished physically to dissect a body to learn how it was made... ouch!... imagine... taking a sharp knife in one's hand and beginning to slice a cadaver... a *female* cadaver! Sacrilege. I heard Leonardo once sat in an infirmary three days waiting for a woman to die so he could claim her body for his dismembering purposes.... unfathomable. I am not the cerebral Pallas whom those two worshipped; I am the goddess of Love! Neither my Praxiteles, nor Apelles cut up any cadavers. Nor did Raphael, heaven bless him. And he did very well without these indecorous surgeries. As well as the other two did, in my unhumble opinion. It was the intuitive part of his physical appreciation of the female form, which was ardent to say the least, that mattered. (The other two preferred the male form). It made him the supreme master of a female nude, the Praxiteles of the post-classical world. He once mentioned to a friend (who dutifully wrote it down for your benefit) that, like the masters of classical antiquity, he had been unable to find any one model of sufficient beauty, but had used the best parts of several, among them, certainly Praxiteles's Knidian and Botticelli's Venus. His Galatea is the Knidian that moves, holding the reins and in charge of her own destiny, while turning around in a brilliant corkscrew pose to look up at her creator (creator of us all!), as if to say 'thank you' and 'goodbye.' Her brilliant blood-red chlamys blows around her, as she firmly stands inside Botticelli's shell, made over into a real craft with two paddle wheels attached for faster progress, and propelled not by ethereal winds, but by very real dolphins, while surrounded by marine courtiers. And where is she sailing now? Let me tell you—she is sailing to Venice this time, for in Venice other men anticipate her, knees trembling and hearts palpitating, ready to worship her, love her, and ... For boys will be boys.

Giorgione must have liked the idea of a sleeping Beauty better than an active one, and at a touch of his magic brush, I went back to sleep. In his version, called Giorgione's Venus, I seem "poured out" onto the receptive and generous earth; my gestures are unconscious caresses. He lulled me to sleep in the shadow of a jagged outcropping and made me dream of old joys, protected by nothing but fragile twigs and offshoots that spring from the rock above my head, with a distant village in the background. Clever man, Giorgione—as I sleep (and only when I sleep!), I am unaware of my beauty, of my nudity; unaware of being observed. But I am very aware of this while looking at the picture... Ah!—look at me, honorable Reader—I am so lovely, so alive, forever immortal of course; just as in a fairy tale. A male fantasy. But fantasy only, for no male, earthly or deific, can dare disturb me. My pose is calm and natural, and it escapes one at first how like the Knidian I am. In Giorgione's version, I have made a bed for myself out of my chlamys, while as the Knidian I was laying it aside before a ritual bath, and the gentle and elongated delicacy of my Giorgione's form lacks the mature solidity of the antique shape. But if it is true that classical beauty depends on a perfect ease of transition from one lucid shape to another (as a great antiquarian once said), then my Giorgione version is as classically beautiful as the Knidian ever was.

But once having been awoken, Beauty cannot go back to sleep for long. It is decreed that she must be roused by a prince, however many disguises he may assume, and in Venice the prince assumed the disguise of Tiziano Vecellio, known to posterity as Titian. If ever there was a prince of princes, Titian was that prince. It was said of him that when Emperor Charles V visited his studio, the emperor bent down to pick up a brush dropped by Titian. My divine grapevine has it that an identical story was told about Apelles and Alexander the Great. That time Alexander did the bending. If history can repeat itself, so can its heroes. And its Aphrodites.

These days, honorable Reader, as you well know, copying someone's design is called plagiarism; back in the Renaissance (as in all ages except yours), it was called inspiration. My marvelous Giorgione lines, as sweeping as the curves of hills or river currents, were imitated again and again, and no one's eyebrow arched when Titian made them his own. Fully awake I am  this time. Oh, and how! I am no longer part of an undulating landscape. I *am* the undulating landscape, placed firmly in the interior of a sumptuous and sensuous room, in the middle of a sumptuous and sensuous bed, where, let's face it, as a goddess of Love, I sumptuously and sensually belong. In form, I am almost identical to Giorgione's vision of me, but only in form; and form, as we know, is skin-deep, however deep the skin.

There is no trace of unawareness in this version of me, no inhibition. Indeed, even though Titian's adaptation is called *Venus of Urbino*, no one seems to know who the model is. Even I don't know. I must have been elsewhere being painted by someone else, while this one was being painted by Titian. Is she someone's future wife? mistress? Most likely a mistress, since, presumably, a young girl intended for marriage in the sixteenth century would not be posing nude before her fiancée's painter, even if the painter be Titian. On second thought, Titian may be an exception. If an emperor could bend down to pick up his brushes for him, a blushing bride of another man could strip her garments for him. But she is probably a mistress. And a mistress who is not only inviting, but beckoning, with her left hand not only *not* hiding (as my Knidian did), but indicating, the source of pleasure. This part of classical nudes' female anatomy, you might know, Reader, was never portrayed with pubic hair, which is why, perhaps, Titian placed a fern of uncertain plucked carnal semblance in her right hand. Her lips are tempting, her eyes encouraging. I know for a fact that wealthy men (who *will* be boys) kept similar paintings in their bedrooms (which were separate from their wives' bedrooms, if they had wives) to enhance physical desire, which their wives, whom they married for their property, did not. In the same fashion, Last Suppers were painted in monasteries' dining refectories to enhance spiritual hunger. They both stimulated appetite. Last Suppers tickled pious buds, and the paintings in question did the job with the less pious. Some six—seven hundred years later, certain moving images on electronic equipment would be employed for a similar purpose. I happen to find the Titian option more elegant.

Venus of Urbino is a supreme achievement of coyness and seduction, with the sleeping dog at her feet accentuating both sentiments. If ever one indulged in the attainment of carnal knowledge (or perfection thereof) with a dog present, staring, and barking occasionally, one must know the odd feeling of uneasiness, for although dogs presumably do not share human (or divine) sensations, when it comes to carnal knowledge, one feels they might, and thus the sense of *in flagrante delicto* is uncomfortably there, even if the "there" is canine. It took Titian, of course, subtle and wicked at once, to exploit this titillating paradox, as he tied up the curtain behind the girl in a loose knot ready to be undone at any wanton moment, in order to separate her from the background handmaidens when the curtain is drawn, but the pooch will remain. The pooch, and whoever she is looking at so beguilingly, who will be untying the knot. All sorts of knots. The pooch, needless to say, will wake up with the commencement of procedures, and will bark.

Yes, a supreme achievement she is indeed, of stimulating nature. And one never stops with supreme achievements of stimulating nature, particularly when one is a genius, and when significant commissions are to be made on further achievements, and Titian was not only a brilliant and intuitive painter, but a brilliant and intuitive businessman as well. To be sure, if he was sometimes less than admirable, it was because he had an unpleasantly calculating side, scheming ruthlessly for preferment, lucrative sinecures, and commissions. He flattered to the limit his royal patrons (while they were bending for his brushes), bargained for prices, and let himself be puffed egregiously by blackguard friends. But you see, this side of his character was eminently Venetian. The inhabitants of La *Serenissima always* schemed for splendor and pleasure, measuring even their indulgences, which was how they made their city great, and Titian was nothing if not Venetian, with the capacity for both passion and affairs. He had no desire—no more than Raphael did—to cut anyone's departed flesh. He wished to cut their overstuffed money bags while they were very much alive, and he worked hard to get what he wanted. To Raphael, it all came effortlessly.

Once other men saw *La Urbina*, they wanted one too. Consequently, Titian reproduced her in the guise of more Venuses, and Dianas, and Eves, and most notably, Danaës. Nothing like a respectable mythological context to excuse a disrespectable erotic content. Titian loved the story of Danaë most particularly. This gorgeous princess of Argos had a nitwitted father who had locked her in a dungeon away from male eyes, and from male everything else, lest she should bear a child who would slay the grandfather (so it was foretold). But prophesy or not, the fool should have known that lust could never be censored! I make certain it can't. Sure enough, the all-seeing and all-hearing Great Clamorer heard her sobs, loved her looks, and presently visited her in the disguise of a golden shower, with which said Clamorer

(aka Zeus) fertilized her princely ovum, producing the hero Perseus. Once grown, in addition to all sorts of other achievements, he also, although unwittingly, dispatched his grandfather. Just as well—the world is weighed down with enough fools.

At least four large canvases exist from Titian's own hand, all portraying Danaë in an attitude of eagerness and excitement, her body expectantly turned toward her Olympian lover, mouth open, legs open, everything open, left hand on the same left thigh as *La Urbina's*, but deeper thrust, gold rain following the hand. This is the next stage in the private life of *La Urbina*. Even the dog visibly continues his existence with at least one Danaë, while with others, where he is not visible, he is hiding under the covers, what with all the commotion.

The older Titian got (and he'll get very ancient), the more insatiable he became with his nudes, and the more salacious. Observe the stunning princess of Phoenicia, Europa by name, as she is being abducted by the aforementioned Zeus, who clearly had his fill of Danaë and went elsewhere for excitement, this time to the Mediterranean's eastern shores, disguised as a Big Bad Bull, to woo her. In this camouflage,  he had a silken white pelt, golden horns, and his breath emanated saffron crocus. The princess must have liked what she saw and smelt, because, with no further ado, and with a premonition of further delights, she presently climbed onto the Big Bad Bull's Back and sailed off to Crete, limbs ajar to receive enough of the aforementioned delights to procreate the whole European population.

His hoary soul excited by this apparition, Titian not only brought passion into art. He brought something else. By this time in his life—he wasn't young, you know, about eighty when he painted Europa, which is a lot in human years—his vision was impaired by a disorder I remember described in Hippocratic writings (I read all sorts of miscellany when I am bored) as a blinding disease occurring most commonly in the elderly, and it said that once the pupil has the color of the sea, eyesight is impaired and one will often find that the other eye is also impaired. It was called glaucoma back then, and is still called glaucoma. Reason I remember it so well (I usually forget most of what I read), is that I was born of the sea, and know better than anyone that the sea has many colors. I was therefore greatly puzzled that this great man who coined the Hippocratic Oath, this paragon of ancient medicine, this scientist who summed up the medical knowledge of all previous schools, prescribing practices for all physicians to follow, should be so inaccurate about such a simple thing as the color, or rather colors, of the sea... Which color (or combination thereof) could he possibly mean? I remember mentioning this to Hephaestus, my husband, but he told me not to worry my pretty head about things I could never understand, flexed his huge biceps and hobbled back into his forge. I then asked Ares when he visited me one night, while Hephaestus was in his forge flexing his huge biceps, but Ares told me I shouldn't think too much as it might hurt me. He told me I was made for other things, demonstrated what they were, and was off presently to slaughter more foes and obliterate more enemies. Men, whether human or divine, are odd creatures indeed. They consider women lesser beings, yet give us useless counsel, thus leaving us to our own devices.

Well, nothing was left for me to do, but to fare for myself, which I did, and I think what really happened was that Titian explained Hippocrates much better than Hippocrates explained himself, at least in art terms, and however unwittingly, leaped ahead of his time. Reader, you know about Impressionism and Expressionism because they happened before your lifetime, but Titian would have no idea about the worthy Isms, since his lifetime happened four hundred years before they came about, yet he ushered them both into being long before those other men had a hand at them. He did both—dissolved form (as the professional jargon goes), *and* expressed his intemperate enthusiasm. The first he did through execution, which was a function of the venerable artist's impaired sight. Just look at the picture—the sea is not one color, it's multiple colors! All blended together. There'll be another painter, four hundred years later, called Monet. He also lived a long time, with the same impact of years on his vision. And everyone knows what *he* did with colors. Of course everyone knows—he is in every museum and half-museum around the world, and no wonder—splash, splash and the painting was done—he produced legions of them. To think what people pay for them these days. What fools these mortals be. So much for Impressionism. Yet, Titian, unlike Monet, did spend many days and months on *his* paintings. The second "ism" —Expressionism—he easily achieved through content, which was a function of his profligate old soul. Should anyone like to partake, one will find both Europa and her Big Bad Bull in Boston's Isabella Gardner Museum. But I must stop rambling, as my husband would say (the one in the forge with the biceps), and get a move on.

In the following century, another princely painter, Peter Paul Rubens by name, will pick up where Titian left off, inaugurating the age of moist, sumptuous, delectable flesh. At fifty three, he married the sixteen-year-old Hélène Fourment and still full of inexhaustible animal vitality, painted her again and again. (I wish my husband were so loving. Or the lover.) These paintings are both poetic *and* full-blooded tributes to the pleasures—licit pleasures—of the flesh. And why not—a terribly clever mortal by the name of Diderot once said "*Mille peintres sont morts sans avoir senti la chair.*" (Thousands of painters die without having tasted the flesh). And Diderot, having compiled the first Encyclopedia—the anthology of *all* human knowledge—obviously knew what he was talking about, for plenty of his encyclopedist friends must have been in the same predicament as the *mille*

peintres, dying without having tasted the flesh. Diderot was clearly not one of them, having produced a daughter. I can't imagine when he found time or energy though, what with all the other field study required by multiple subjects in his Encyclopedia. On the other hand, in my celestial opinion, even if lots of painters did not die without having tasted the flesh, they were not necessarily capable of rendering it while they lived.

Well, Rubens not only tasted it in all varieties, but was

unequivocally capable of rendering it. One of my absolute favorites is the one he did of Hélène Fourment, *à la Knidian* (I always like the ones made after me the best), having lovingly wrapped her exposed flesh in a luxurious fur against winter chills. This was the North, after all, and my Greek chlamys was insufficient in Flemish temperatures. Besides, the intimate sensation of texture, which makes the contact of the fur to Hélène's skin so stimulating, is there to make up for my sweeping nudity in the Knidian—*chacun à son goût.* And Rubens's taste was very obvious—he painted his young wife as a cornucopia of ampleness—a thanksgiving for abundance. The wrinkles and puckers of her delicate pink skin, which I find adorable, and he obviously did too, are the extra protection against those objectionable boreal winds. Yes, she is rotund. Of course she is rotund—thin girls could not long survive in Antwerp in the days before central heating! When I look at my nude statues in those northern museums (and some of them are outside, in the gardens!), I shiver head to toe just looking at them. It was so easy for me, on my warm Mediterranean island, to take off my chlamys and step into a bath whenever the desire struck me. The River Schelt, linked to the Northern Sea, did not allow similar luxury. We must all admit (I before anyone else) that in transferring my Knidian ideal from the southern shores to the north, Rubens conceived a new woman in art by giving her carnal reality, for even Titian's beauties retained a divine element. But Rubens did something else. He knew that it's with the eyes that intimacy begins. Titian knew it too, and had deliberately given *La Urbina* the expression of self-conscious eroticism. But Rubens—ah!—dear worshipper—he had given his Hélène the eyes of a woman in love—sensual yet sincere, bashful yet inviting, the eyes of a shy ingénue enamored with her husband; innocent, trusting, adoring, ready to drop this voluptuous fur at a moment's notice and make him the happiest of men, while he made her the happiest of women. A glorious, intimate picture, never meant for the public eye. Only for Him and for Her. I visit him often in Elysian Fields, and each time he tells me how unhappy he is that this painting is in a museum. He doesn't mind others, but that this one is exposed to the public eye, he finds to be an invasion of privacy; he finds it invidious.

At this point, dear Reader, I feel I must quickly count my stock before proceeding further. When awoken by Botticelli towards the end of the 15th century, I was fully a goddess, just as I was a thousand years earlier as the Knidian. When I was admired by Raphael and Titian in the 16th century, my goddess-like aspect began to take on the carnal attributes of a female. When worshipped by Rubens in the 17th century, whose goddesses were immortal females, and whose females were mortal goddesses, there was never a hint of vulgarity, for all the overflowing flesh. I became fully a woman, although still godlike. But of course you know that what made us, gods, approach human level, was an element of human nature in us, not so much as a hint of divine in you, unless you came fully to appreciate us. Me in particular.

Alas, my godlike aspects will begin to disappear in the 18th century, when it was bad form to take anything seriously, until heads began to roll, which was taken very seriously. Up until the reign of Mademoiselle Guillotine, however, Monsieur Boucher held sway, and combining the back view of the Knidian, which so delighted the ancient visitor to my shrine on the Isle of Knidos, with the front view of Europa, which proved so inspirational to Titian many centuries later, he offered his own view—of several of his king's mistresses, to his king's delight. The back view predominated. For whatever inexplicable reason, in the *dix-huitième*, as the 18th century

came to be known, the preferred aspect of a female form was from behind, in the mood of undisguised eroticism, or should we say, of open lust. Boucher painted a number of those views, most notably the Blond Odalisque and the Brown Odalisque. The model for the Blond was a certain Miss O'Murphy, whose round young limbs, as they sprawled with undisguised satisfaction on the cushions of her sofa, Boucher had enabled the viewer to enjoy with as little shame as she was enjoying herself. The viewer at the time was the King himself, whose mistress Miss O'Murphy was. She wasn't his only mistress, naturally, the oldest and most beloved being Madame de Pompadour. As age crept in and changed Madame's appearance, however, she became the king's best friend and also his procuress, as only a loving and understanding woman could be. It was she who introduced the king to Miss O'Murphy. The king's satisfaction must have been of a dual nature—that of seeing young flesh as a matter of course, but also of the middle-aged man's pleasure in the knowledge that he could still satiate a very young woman. Kings too will be boys.

The Brown Odalisque was beyond any undisguised eroticism and/or open lust – she was, and still is, an avatar of carnality. The model, I must inform you, was on rather intimate terms with the painter; so intimate, in fact, that he no longer felt the need to constrain his feelings with any degree of refinement, and we are full force in the world of sin. Never mind the chlamys  that I, as the Knidian, had taken off to step into my bath; never mind the fur that kept Hélène Fourment warm and beloved; never mind even the luxurious cushions that gave support to the delicately titillating Miss O'Murphy. This one wears a scanty silk under-dress, which she does not care to undress. While lying on her stomach, she pulls this under-dress up with the inviting insouciance of a mature hussy, allowing the viewer to evaluate her body with the same degree of appraisal that he would a horse (slapping the flank not out of the question). How far have the mighty fallen!

One wonders whether Boucher was in any way influenced by discoveries in the recently unearthed Pompeii. In its proportion of bordellos to its population, no city of the Roman Empire could vie with Pompeii, and these bordellos' interiors were covered with meticulous pictorial depiction of human activity that went on within these interiors. When brought to light and cleaned up, these images were met with howls of outraged propriety on the part of an eighteenth century Christendom that believed in redemption through modesty, and with peals of delighted hilarity on the smaller part that believed in redemption through sin. Boucher, naturally, belonged to the latter category and acted accordingly. But here is the ruse—it seems the model for the Brown Odalisque was his wife... at least so goes the gossip, which we must always believe (you may recollect how much *I* love and believe in gossip), although extant portraits of Mme Boucher show neither brown complexion, nor penchant for flagrant exhibitionism. And the face is very different. But the whole definition of a 'nude' never took *face* into account back then—it concentrated on the *body*, and the face could always be substituted with a formula that was ever ready at hand. Still, if indeed the body is that of Madame, she and Monsieur must have shared the greatest sense of humor, only possible with an unusual degree of understanding, very different indeed from Sir Peter Paul and his Hélène. I do, of course, know the truth, but there are certain truths that even goddesses are not at liberty to divulge. Yet this I can tell you—whatever was Madame and Monsieur's personal relationship, when it came to commissions from princes and princesses, Monsieur always delivered a princely product, as expected of princely artists in the tradition of Titian and Rubens.

But all must come to an end, and France rolled into (and through) the 19th century atop toppled thrones, decapitated heads and broken barricades. Princes disappeared, and princely artists disappeared with them. Bourgeois artists came in their stead, delivering the bourgeois product for the bourgeois public. This public, de facto, had simpler tastes than aristocrats of yore, but they pretended they didn't, and their favorite painters pretended they didn't either, no matter how smoothed out their forms and waxen their surfaces. With few exceptions, there was little charm and less passion; mechanical adherence to academic staples had removed the last tremors of excitement. It was this self-satisfying pretence at legitimacy and decorum in both art and circumstance that received so painful a shock from Manet's Olympia. The age of *épater les bourgeois* was launched—once again Aphrodite was awakened, but she didn't like it this time. Because now she was a thorn in one's side rather than a delight in one's eye and/or various other parts of one's anatomy. And to be named *Olympia...* after my dwelling place... Reader—not entirely devoid of a sense of humor, I can appreciate a witticism, but cynicism is another thing altogether. Cynicism, to the horror of all of us Olympians, was originated by that mad *Diogenes* of Sinope, who preached that one must perform, in public, all bodily functions that should be done in private. He renounced all possessions, lived in a filthy barrel, and never washed. And he stunk... oh, dear Reader, did he stink! We could smell the stench all the way up on our glorious Mount, and were it not for the intoxicating redolence of wild poppies, which we used as air freshener, our lives would have been impossible. You therefore must sympathize with my distress on seeing cynicism, albeit transformed and reconstructed, manifested again, after over two thousand years, in this creature of *Monsieur* Manet's.

If anyone could predict that in less than fifty years after its scandalous unveiling, *Olympia*, this unspeakable hussy, would knock at the doors of the Louvre and be admitted, such a prophet would have passed for a madman. But she did knock, and she was admitted, and she still resides there (in its *Musée d'Orsay affiliation*), and the trend she inaugurated was, for a moment, called Intimism, which appellation was presently lost among all the other 'isms' that the era produced. This Intimism had nothing to do with the lovely intimacy of Rubens's young wife, but rather with this new cynical appetite for indecent exposure as a tool to shock bourgeoisie out of its complacency. It should have been called Intimidationism. The composition for *Olympia* obviously came from Titian's *La Urbina*, but while Titian clearly found his model alluring, Manet viewed his with something more akin to fascinated dismay and curiosity. Her

form is barely sketched, and instead of a little dog that slept peacefully at the feet of *La Urbina*, there is a hissing, arched black cat at the feet of Olympia, and Manet visibly regarded *him*  with fear, and who wouldn't! Whether or not the animal is a mascot for the lady, the lady seems to have less to do with artistic tradition than with the artist's attitude. In artistic tradition nudes were pink and pliant; Olympia is white and hard. In artistic tradition, nudes were graceful and appealing; Olympia is stiff and awkward. In artistic tradition, nudes softly seduced; this one challenges. Nudes were *nude*, while this one, with her harem slippers and a black ribbon around the neck is *naked*, all the more so for these exiguous accoutrements. And above all, academic nudes never had any particular character, while this one has an unmistakable character of a dubious sort, and is distinctly a someone. Indeed all the signs pointed to one of Paris's expensive houses of ill-repute, which every self-respecting bourgeois regularly attended (including *Monsieur* Manet who died of syphilis), and just as regularly pretended they didn't. Prudery and transgression were perfect chums behind the scenes of Second Empire Paris, so long as the latter wasn't shoved in the face of the former. How dare *Monsieur* Manet offend the delicacy of the *bien élevé* by doing so ... Whereas La Urbina laid a delicate hand upon her source of pleasure, La Olympia covers hers with a firm hand, her face indicating that it is a source of income before pleasure, and that she should prefer payment before delivery. Whereas La Urbina dangled a tasteful fern in her right hand, which may, or may not have referred to the androgenic thatch always tastefully shaved off in classical nudes, La Olympia's black maid shoves an odorous bouquet into one's face, each flower promising a surrogate delight. Black maids, when available, were employed to give a sense of exoticism to the establishment; whether or not they habitually offered fragrant blossoms to male clientele, and whether they offered these blossoms on behalf of their mistresses, or their own, male clientele alone knew, and I am not about to tell.

Once the house of ill repute entered art full-force, it will never leave, and every salacious, smutty and wanton exertion within its walls will be examined, scrutinized and dissected in the name of depravity, also known as open-mindedness. Few artists were as open-minded as Pablo Picasso, who did his own take on the subject. The curtain that so decoratively hung over La Urbina's head is now pulled over by a fearsome creature of odious appearance, and we are in the presence of *Demoiselles d'Avignon* of one of

Barcelona's notorious brothels that served this vigorous port's vigorous mariners, and, evidently, some vigorous painters as well. There are five of these sirens in his picture, the first one (counting left to right) pulling the curtain. They are so execrable, they fail to embarrass, as Boucher's Brown Odalisque does. Once pulled, the curtain reveals two vixens in the center and two monstrosities on the right. I just overheard a conversation in the gallery, between two men who seem to me very familiar; but for their mode of dress, they could easily be the ones who asked to see me in my shrine on Knidos two and a half millennia ago. One was tall, bald, and thin, the other short, hairy and rotund.

Bald—Are they standing or lying, these two phantoms in the center?

Hairy—Looks like a vertical idea of a horizontal intent.

Bald—That's funny. You mean lying down *à la* Olympia, or standing up *à la* Knidian, arms raised this time??

Hairy—I suppose if it worked for Picasso, it should work for us.

Bald—But the other two fearsome apparitions on the right, as hideous as Hell is Deep—do you think they might be the black attendants on the two Olympias in the center?

Hairy—Possible ...

Bald—Where are the flowers?

Hairy—Down below.

Bald—No, that's a still-life of some suggestive fruit.

Hairy—There isn't much left to suggestion here.

Bald—Look at this ghoul in the front right squatting in a corkscrew contortion. What on earth is the meaning of this?

Hairy—Picasso must not have wished to impoverish the picture by representing what he saw directly, which was 180 degrees of her. He obviously wanted to represent what he knew of her as well, and he knew 360 degrees of her—her front and back views, as well as horizontal and vertical sections.

Bald—You mean the vertical idea of a horizontal intent?

Hairy—Ditto.

Bald—How well did he know these sections?

Hairy—Very well indeed, I should think. And so you see, why not indicate them on canvas as well. Besides, economy is in order. Both sides of her face are alike, if one can call this a face. But no matter—give the contour of one side full face, and show that the head has a back, by doing the other contour in profile. Set the whole thing on the frontal view of her rear, so to speak, make her squat, and god (or a mariner), only knows what pleasures are in store, both visually and sensually. Not to mention financially.

Bald—To the painter or the establishment?

Hairy—Oh, to the painter to be sure. Much, much more to the painter. Laughed all the way to the bank, I wager, while Matisse cried.

Bald—His heirs are still laughing, presumably.

Hairy—Hm. Look at it—a triumph of hate is this picture - of hate and of triumph! – an incensed howl against the eternal feminine. Which is why Matisse cried—because with this, Picasso beat him to the inauguration of 20th century art. You can read more about it in a delightful little volume called "Artravesty;" it's the third article, titled *Mona Lisa vs. Modern American Womanhood*.

Bald—I thought we were in it too.

Hairy—Yes, we are the second and the longest article.

And now I'll tell you, Reader, how all this happened. This picture took a singular inspiration, a stimulant that disallowed anything as prosaic as just ugly women. Matisse had already painted those in bushels, winning kudos from enamored votaries therewith, which meant (in the context of the disintegrating world of the turn of the century) that Picasso had to go beyond what Matisse had done. It was competition to the death—to the death of art as I loved it, alas! Picasso needed some formula for the treatment of the body that owed nothing whatever to classical tradition, which was difficult to find, for even Shiva and Lakshmi were love-linked to my Athens. Fortuitously, the first ever comprehensive show of Negro sculpture was mounted at the Trocadero at the time, and *there* the bleeding stigmata struck our challenger. At last, here was a totally non-Grecian depiction of the body, the kind of image that would surely *épater les bourgeois* more scandalously than anything prior had ventured, and, just as importantly, would reduce Matisse to his own paint dust. It was irresistible. As his vixen lifted the curtain, Picasso opened the flood gate.

Bald—But for how long? Everyone knows jungle cannot replace the Acropolis. He did go back to the academics of course.

49

Hairy—Of course he did. All the better ones did. And this one was very good. He knew how to exploit current trends, how to use ignorance, delusion and affectation of the public bored with tradition and seeking escapes. He knew this public wished for nefarious emotions finally offered for exhibit by the breakdown of established conventions, and he delivered *à la carte*. His art, because distorted in itself, had a desired distorting effect on the viewer. And as the viewer wanted MORE, he kept delivering to taste, soon becoming the arbiter of taste, after which he could do no wrong. No matter how brief or tentative his next experiment, it was presently acclaimed sublime by the chic and the literati. But he himself knew that avant-garde art ages rapidly, while Old Master art is ageless. The word *avant-garde*, remember, comes from vanguard, the leading contingent in a military formation and the first to perish from enemy attack. In the end, the creator of Demoiselles became sort of a radical traditionalist, realizing that traditional art would always be more radical, durable, and consequential than avant-garde, which, in the last analysis, had no lasting human value let alone lasting aesthetic appeal. It only has credibility and value as part of the historical record, as period art and a symptom of the destructiveness of the modern Zeitgeist.

Bald—Did you ever see Otto Dix's version of la Urbina? It's called *Reclining Woman on Leopard Skin*, and she glares at you out of her fierce feline eyes, seemingly ready to spring and tear you apart with her claw-like right hand.

Hairy—Ha! Yes, and she has an assistant, too, all set to help her. Instead of *La Urbina's* pooch or even the less agreeable cat that accompanied *Olympia*, this one has a scary monster for a pet, a bloodcurdling combination of a wild cat, jackal, gargoyle... no one knows what else, hissing at the intruder, sharp teeth bared and tiny eyes bloodshot. Both, the mistress and the pet, are provocative monsters, and a charming pair they make, a true sight for our lecherous male eyes.

Bald—Lecherous to be sure. How the tastes have changed, eh?

Hairy—Yes, if we trust Otto Dix and his tigress, they certainly have done.

Bald—Then again, there is something androgynous in that harpy, don't you think?

Hairy—You mean the viewer, at this age of ours, could be a female? Indeed, many are in fact, which does of course add an extra disreputable touch to the picture, as if anything 'extra' is needed. But whoever the viewer is, the creature, in her animal crouch creating an odd fusion of repulsion and seduction, opulence and vulgarity, is ready for sadistic action. Are *you* ready??

Honorable Reader—I don't know about you, but I do know about me, and I am certainly not ready for anything of the sort. I therefore should perhaps bring this discourse to a close, because, even though I could scribble on, my subject assumes only more alarming an aspect as I write, which I find disagreeable. But I shall not conclude without recapitulating.

Greeks wished to perpetuate my body because it was beautiful. They perfected the nude that men might feel like gods. Rome, seduced by Hellenic grace out of her hoary Puritanism and her ignorance of refinements, embraced whole-heartedly the charm of foreign spells, and again I was worshiped. With time, although not until her Empire had swallowed up the despotism of her paterfamilias, the best of Roman matrons were the spectacle of delicacy, culture, wit, beauty and ease united in a woman, and that woman was a woman of the world.

Then darkness descended. A new god appeared, an incomprehensible and intolerant one, who denied all other gods, who denied me, who denied life itself... He believed that the world was to end, and thus spoke against love, passion, against all things human that make humans divine. He wished humans debased and celibate, with only himself for a stern and implacable master. The punishment of the damned is inability to love, and in the bleak burgs, among squalid ignorance and abysmal barbarism, a loveless man was scared out of his wits, and, Reader, I was scared too, which is why I went into a millenarian slumber, for there are no rational forces on earth, or on Olympus, that can combat the irrational ones. We tried—for very many centuries we tried, and the Greeks tried too, but we lost.

Yet the world did not end, and despite the new god's denial of my existence, I lived on, asleep, until awoken. And when awoken, I learned that the new god had become very old, and that all his teeth had fallen out due to scurvy, since he denied the pleasure of eating citrus, as he denied the pleasure of knowing me. Toothless and wrinkled, he became much older than I will ever be, for in bringing eternal joy, I will be eternally young. This new god was so old that he was pronounced dead by someone, I forget who. He had come in preaching gloom, woe and poverty—the three sure recipes for rapid aging. But I came back as fresh and radiant as ever I was at the time when a puzzled Pygmalion, uncertain whether the independent form of his creation really excelled the living woman, wished for the woman. And you remember, Reader, that the story of Pygmalion was based on my Praxiteles.

And now dear Reader, having taken so much of your time, and feeling that I may no longer, in fairness, presume of your patience, I shall conclude as economically and succinctly as I can.

After the glory of Greece and Rome, and after many centuries of darkness, when I was no longer, in Florence, the Flower City, *joie d'amour* and *joie de vivre* were reborn, as I was reborn, and the suave perfume of civilization was resummoned. In Florence, which rose out of medieval bewilderment as I had once arisen out of the sea foam, I was awoken, and I held sway, in one form or another, for the next five hundred years. But dear-oh-dear, the suave perfume, which in its first fragrance mended manners, with time turned acid and ended by dissolving morals. Decadence had crept in, and with it, the delusion of the mind, disillusion of the soul, and, worst of all, dissolution of me. And I cannot help but bemoan this so-called "creative spasm," and what I feel to be just the lack of judgment and understanding, despite their creators pretending intellectualistic exercises thereby. And these exercises, which, I have no doubt, are of great importance to their practitioners, are hardly understandable to the rest of the world, lest the rest of the

Mona Lisa vs. Modern American Womanhood

I was once present at a conversation between three American males, all married to European females (two of the three men having contracted themselves in this fashion a couple of times to two different countries consecutively). During this conversation relative merits of an American vs. a European female upbringing were discussed, the latter declared preferable, and unconvincing reasons for similar preference were unconvincingly stated. An appeal was then made to me to attempt to state the differences with more compelling arguments, which was an awkward request, as being a female of a decidedly European upbringing, yet having happily lived the greater part of my life in America and tightly keeping my carefully manicured grip on an American passport, I was loath to pass judgment on either side of the Big Blue Divide. There were other considerations of course, having to do with the all too well known pitfalls of clichés and stereotypes.

There was also the feeling that the conversation could be construed as sexist by non-participants (particularly female non-participants), but as all three men were charming ladies' men who had a natural love and appreciation of women (and were beloved by women), the "sexist" epithet didn't fit. In the situation, "sexy" was more appropriate. All three were urbane and cultivated representatives of the previous generation of Americans, deeply patriotic, although schooled in European establishments, where whatever remained of chivalry after the two great wars, was erratically introduced into their own upbringing, and now uncertainly permeated the air of the conversation and confounded their judgment in the context of the significantly changed attitudes of the twenty first century. Too mature and set in their own ways for significant change, yet too intelligent not to be aware of it, they looked to me with the disarming allure of secure and solid men in need of clarification. I was more charmed than offended by this appeal; judging was out of the question. Pressure was on.

The only way I thought I could handle this pressure, as well as try to avoid the aforementioned clichés and stereotypes, was to turn to history for assistance, most particularly to history's hand maiden, art history. Art is ever an incontrovertible determinant of human experience, autonomous of fads, whims and politics, because it is an honest manifestation of human mind and an earnest expression of human soul, independently of human artifice. As John Ruskin once said, "Great nations write their autobiographies in three manuscripts—the book of their deeds, the book of their words and the book of their art... of the three the only trustworthy one is the last." Summoning art as a visual manifestation of sexual magnetism through time seemed a right thing to do. Procreative activity is a thing of nature. Human love is a thing of civilization. Neither human love nor human civilization is flawless, as humans are not flawless, which is a blessing. Each time men have tried perfection, disasters ensued, because the most horrible of all delusions is belief in one's virtue. I hope to god I am not thus delusional, which is in itself an arrogant claim I suppose. Therefore, with the understanding that in evoking human art I also demonstrate my flawed human interpretation of it, with which many may disagree, here goes.

▼

There is no doubt in anyone's mind that at the end of a century-long struggle for equality, western women have emerged victorious. One of this race myself, and knowing something of history, I cannot but greatly appreciate the change. There is, however, a question (continuously debated), whether, in having acquired tangible male rights, many a woman may not have lost sight of some intangible female privileges, which often served them in good stead in the days of old, but to which they are no longer entitled by virtue of equality. For my part, I think the advantages gained far outweigh the ones lost, but the platitude remains that with time one tends to take the gains for granted, while waxing nostalgic for the privileges no longer within reach. The next obvious and entirely human platitude (and feminine into the bargain), is to wish to have her man and rule him too, which is rarely, if ever, possible. Hence the perennial issue of balance, and, unavoidably, of femininity vs. feminism.

Having been born in Russia, which country had remained medieval long after the West moved toward modernity, and which, in some respects, is still deeply feudal, I have often been amused at the contempt with which Russian women regard the word "feminist." To the majority of them, it is an insult. Why be equal to men when they can have them at their feet.

French and Italian women, on the other hand, relying on their millenarian tradition of manipulating men in every direction, while allowing them to remain 'superior,' or at least to think they are, have found an easy balance, and are no worse for wear. Same, I suppose, could be said of the rest of Europe, with regional peculiarities playing their part.

This leaves America, and here, it seems, the problem escalates. With no sustained experience of maneuvering behind the throne, American women often fall into the black & white pitfall of Penthouse vs. Powerhouse, and, from what I've observed, are happy or secure in neither. Which is why I thought I'd write this essay.

Before I begin, though, I must make a disclaimer that, while I strongly feel that in broad terms what I am about to say applies to the general majority of American femalehood, it is by no means definitive in particulars. It certainly does not apply to *my* American women friends. *My* American women friends, in point of fact, have what many European women sadly lack—honesty, integrity and candor. Artlessness in the best of senses.

▼

In keeping my word to the three American males, I shall be evoking four very familiar female images from the world of art that, having long lost their novelty with the tedium of widespread usage, are today taken for granted and no longer contemplated. But contemplated they must be if one is to hold on to the tenuous claim of calling oneself human. The two earlier ones (Leonardo and Giorgione) are my steady companions, used more than once in this volume. The later ones I like less, and I go into endless lengths throughout this

volume to explain why I like them less. The first one is the *Mona Lisa,* or *La Gioconda,* as she is known outside the English speaking world; she is first because she is most human. Her face, which is by no means beautiful, (at least not overtly so), shines with inner light unimaginable. The rich, somber cloth of her dress is the only indicator of her affluence, for, sitting before a most sublime landscape of the Alpine Dolomites, she wears not a single piece of jewelry. She is the human embodiment of that landscape and needs no further adornment. *She* is the jewel of that landscape. Fully aware of being so, she smiles the primordial smile not of mystery, as it is commonly described, but of knowledge—Permanence disdaining Transience.

Her information and understanding had been formed after the precepts of the Greeks, who knew best, and in accordance with Renaissance principles, which recognized that the Greeks knew best. Her mind, in short, was honed according to the Laws of Nature and outside man's immediate concerns. What Leonardo portrayed, is a supremely *confident* Renaissance woman; one who had acquired superior knowledge based not on quotidian paraphernalia, but on universal understanding. Hence the smile. However much Leonardo, as an artist, may have cared for visual effect, it is definitely the mind behind the face that fascinated him in this model, and the wisdom thereof. It is the knowledge outside petty humanity that makes her most human, most woman, most desirable to those who share her values. Indeed, those who do must love her. Those who don't must *ipso facto* resent her. In either case, understanding this fact is a prerequisite to understanding the face. Without it, *She* cannot be fathomed, however much one stares (or is photographed before the picture) during a prescribed visit to the Louvre.

Today, few Americans, male or female, even begin to intimate what those values are, let alone embrace them, because the quality of their schooling, uncertain at best, has taught them that their own value as individuals resides exclusively in their emotions, and anything that interferes with it, be it an informed reflection or an educated analysis, must be shunned. How funny was Oscar Wilde, when he mocked this emerging tendency a hundred years ago, by making Lady Bracknell say "I do not approve of anything that tampers with natural ignorance. Ignorance is like a delicate, exotic fruit. Touch it, and the bloom is gone." Well, some Americans may not know who Oscar Wilde is, and all of them have long won their political independence from the mother country, but they certainly remained deferential to it in spirit, and, cheerfully following in the Brits' wake, have not only caught up to them in the "ignorance" department, but left them far behind, with the result that now, a century after Lady Bracknell's genial pronouncement, they have successfully accomplished a near loss of the intellectual prerequisites to understand the *Mona Lisa*.

But not to worry, for they have not lost their capacity to understand and appreciate other paintings—those that do not require quite the same cerebral effort—De Kooning's *Woman* for one. This one, bestial, hideous, and vacant, requires no schooling whatever, no brain, and not even a heart on the part of the observer. This particular female of the species, herself lacking both heart and mind, is based on the lowest impulses that originate below the waist, and as such easily identified with. At the time of her creation, the

Americans led the world in tastes and attitudes (as they have done since between the two Great Wars), not the Brits, and it was in America that Holland-born De Kooning achieved his renown, with the ultimate result that his seductresses are selling today for scores of millions of dollars.

More than three hundred years separate Leonardo's Beauty from De Kooning's Beast, in which span of time the plunge from the upper to the nether regions had been accomplished, and applauded by those who accomplished it, beyond redemption. Which makes lingering in the sixteenth century rather than rushing into the twentieth all the more tempting. About the same time as Leonardo was painting his *Mona Lisa*, his younger contemporary, Giorgione, painted the lovely *Sleeping Venus* (illustration in previous article on p. 30). The "Sleeping" part is obvious; the "Venus" is less so, since there isn't a single indication of her divinity in the painting except the landscape which she dominates and personifies as *Mona Lisa* dominates her own landscape. The latter does it with the mind, the former with the body. And what a body....! It moves, undulates, swells and recedes as the landscape moves, undulates, swells and recedes. The two are inseparable; they speak the same language—that of most perfect harmony and sensuality.

Giorgione took Praxiteles's *Knidian Aphrodite* out of her splendid Greek isolation and lay her down in the midst of Veneto's glorious fragrance. And it works! Because "beauty is truth, truth beauty." Harmony, balance, proportion are of Nature and with Nature; they are universal and will work no matter where they are found. Asleep, she is unaware of the observer—the painting is a keyhole peek. And she *does not care*. There can be nothing more natural, more confident, more indifferent to human folly, whatever its guise, than nature's perfect creation participating in nature's celebration. She is a Perfect Nude, above and beyond prudery, shyness, pettiness, strife and/or any other transient concerns.

The same generational gap separates Giorgione from Leonardo as does De Kooning from Picasso; both younger men could be the older men's sons, and in a way they were, in mind, if not in blood. As organic harmony unites the model with the landscape in both sixteenth century paintings, so, in the twentieth century, does orgasmic disharmony unite De Kooning's women with Picasso's *Demoiselles d'Avignon* (previous article p. 48). Leonardo fingerpointed one road to follow, Picasso another. In *Demoiselles,* we are introduced to five uncharming hostesses. The two in the middle attempt, hesitantly, unwillingly, hysterically, to hearken back to Giorgione's reclining model, except no one knows, least of all themselves, whether they are indeed reclining, or perhaps they are standing, or sleeping while standing... Whatever they are doing, they are offering themselves, to men, for they are prostitutes. The painting was originally called *The Brothel of Avignon,* after many similar establishments located on Avinyó Street in Barcelona. Instead of the yielding silken cloth that caresses the body of Giorgione's *Venus*, these harpies are painted against what appears to be broken glass that couldn't possibly be too comfortable considering their profession; and further considering the double weight, the prospect is even more fearful to contemplate. They are given no form, no substance, no knowledge; they can give or receive no true pleasure; their claim to fame is their shock value.

'It is the truth universally acknowledged' that most modern art isn't about the subject, but about the artist. Leonardo's *Mona Lisa* was about the divinity of a beautiful mind and Giorgione's *Venus* about the divinity of a perfect nude. *Demoiselles* is not about the ladies we see on canvas, but about Picasso and *his* state of mind in the historical and cultural context that shaped him. These females have no personalities. They cannot have any, because if they did, they'd overshadow their creator; consequently, they are easily (nay, eagerly) sacrificed on the altar of their creator's ambition.

It is with the three marginal *Demoiselles* that real fun begins. At the time, just prior to painting this thing, the fairly frustrated Picasso was trailing Matisse in shock value, which was then rapidly becoming equivalent  to artistic virtue. While Matisse was indiscriminately throwing wild (fauve) colors onto his canvasses, Picasso was still seemingly locked into his blue/pink sentimentality. This *had* to change. Enter the Trocadero exhibit of sub-Saharan masks that had by then begun to fascinate Europeans because of the preceding century's Scramble for Africa, Social Darwinism, exploration fervor and the like. Our young painter came, he saw, had an epileptic fit... and conquered, by placing the masks atop the three seductresses, while positioning one of them in an obscene squatting pose. He painted three bawdy whores and introduced 'open-mindedness' and 'diversity' into art. Crude and vulgar nakedness replaced sensual and harmonious nudity. In a self-serving attempt to be original and to beat Matisse at outraging the bourgeois, Picasso slid right down to aboriginal. Leo Stein (Gertrude's brother—certainly no bourgeois in spirit) nearly had a heart attack on seeing the thing.

Perhaps because of the lack of a deep artistic tradition of its own, this brief experimental episode in Picasso's very patched career, undertaken exclusively to get ahead of the competition, was taken particularly seriously in America, and American women still live with that experiment, as do their daughters, and their daughters' daughters. No one can definitively tell what the painting is—European? African? Is it front? back? center? Are the bestial test subjects sitting/ standing/ lying/ squatting/ copulating?? There is nothing but uncertainty and bewilderment about the picture that cannot but produce insecurity and self-doubt in its gazers. But never mind; one must admire it, for otherwise one is positively and irrevocably a philistine.

European women, of course, still have their Leonardo, and their Giorgione, and before that their *Knidian*

68

Aphrodite. And in their history they still have such amazing exemplars of womanhood as Madame de Rambouillet and Madame Geoffrin, and Isabella d'Este and Elisabetta Gonzaga, and George Sand and George Elliott, and on and on, till the waters of the Atlantic do us part—a tradition they never renounced, of which they are most proud, and which serves them as the most formidable of foundations. For them, Picasso's *Demoiselles* and De Kooning's *Women* are just a phase that, having served its purpose of amusement and distraction, is then routinely replaced with the universals. Americans do not have the luxury of this tradition; they are taught, ultimately, that modernity is all that matters, and for good reason, since that's when America began to matter. Little wonder that *Demoiselles* and *Women* have become for them definitive in art just as the likes of a Tony Morrison became irrefutable in literature—the latter as questionable a substitute for, say, a George Elliott, as the *Demoiselles* are for Giorgione. Yet, it is *Demoiselles* in art and Ms. Morrison in literature, that are offered as role models. How many here have even heard of George Sand.

Women's Liberation Movement, so beneficial to European women, who succeeded in plucking the best it offered without shedding the best they had, wasn't as kind to many an American woman, who, sinking in the pool of naiveté, aimlessly seized whatever last straw came their way. Lacking a strong tradition of femininity, they haven't valued it. Never having heard of the beautiful Madame du Chatelet who translated and explained Newton to Voltaire, they embraced Margaret Mead. As a result, many of them got saddled with aggression, contentiousness and indifference of taste as character traits, in lieu of poise, dignity and pride of heritage. The exchange has not been to their advantage, for they know not the difference between nakedness and nudity.

What it all comes down to, I suppose, is that however bright and well-meaning the majority of them are, they do not know—were never taught—their own true worth. In fact, they are taught the opposite—not to embrace traditional female values for fear of being taken advantage of by horrible, arrogant males; not to be proud of Western culture (the only culture in the world that gained women their independence!) for fear that this might offend other ethnicities. Today they are taught that African, Amazon, Polynesian, Chinese, Japanese, etc. achievement must be equally considered because it is on par with theirs. Whatever it may be, it is not theirs, and will not support them in their quest for self, which is what one must find before one ventures elsewhere. Is there any wonder they don't know where to turn? How to act? What to learn? Not having a solid platform from which to evaluate anything or anybody, they sink into the tedium of petty concerns and immediate anxieties, made all the worse by innocence and insecurity.

And when married with children, they haven't a clue what to do with the brood. Unqualified to educate them, they raise them. And they try to do good! God knows they try, the conscientious ones: they listen to classical music when pregnant, flash alphabet cards before two-year-old noses, give them music lessons, send them to better schools and go together to the islands... but they don't *think* together; indeed, they think very little. From their culturally needy homes they drive their little Hansels and Gretels into the woods of institutional education to fend for themselves. It is painful to contemplate how many of these children come to resent their parents (something I hear over and over from my students). Very few succeed in destroying the witch and finding the treasure; most gorge themselves on gingerbreads and get eaten by witches. Picasso's and De Kooning's witches.

Meanwhile, *Mona Lisa* smiles.

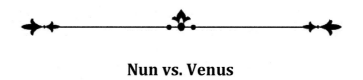

Nun vs. Venus

It is delightful to find an artist in the twentieth century whose work is both distinctly individual yet anchored in the best that humanity had created, for without that anchor we are but driftwood in a turbulent sea. The artist may not be a great artist in the vast scheme of things, but if he is skilled in his craft, intelligently whimsical in his design, unique in his vision, disrespectful of trends and reverent of tradition, he is a winner. Such is Botero, whose imagery is to be admired, for he is a successful interpreter of 'academic' into 'modern.'

What with our own age largely unschooled in the intricacies and historical context of academic art, having opportunely replaced it with modern art that requires no schooling, but which creates a flattering illusion of artistic association, Botero, who spent years in Madrid, most of them in the Prado, Madrid's incomparable museum, found a brilliant formula to 'translate' classical painters that he came to love and understand into modern whimsy. Having found the winning formula, which is proportional exaggeration, he stuck to it with the tenacity of a champion and won both universal kudos and financial rewards.

Please look at the image: Botero's *Nun Eating an Apple*. Lovely, isn't it?

Back in 2007, at Christie's New York, it was estimated to sell for about $300,000 but fetched more than twice that! All right—no more talk of brilliant and glorious *Mona Lisa*, or of hideous *Demoiselles d'Avignon*; let's talk of nuns and of forbidden fruit.

The big question is—What has a nun to do with apples?

Granted, it is a nutritious fruit, and a quick glance at Wikipedia will inform the reader that it is one of the most cultivated tree fruits on earth. Quote: "The proverb 'An apple a day keeps the doctor away', addressing the health effects of the fruit, dates from 19th century Wales. Research suggests that apples may reduce the risk of colon cancer, prostate cancer and lung cancer."

Is it possible our Nun is suffering from one of these? Hardly; certainly not from 'prostate.' She is definitely overweight—there no denying it. Which is a bit of a paradox, because the three essential principles of monasticism (since 6th c. AD) are Poverty (achieved by self-denial), Obedience (achieved by submission), and Celibacy (unachievable). The pleasant roundness of her form pretty much cancels out all likelihood of self-denial (Botero's taste for such forms only confirms it). Obedience is also out, because our Nun looks positively guilty, all the more so for her naughtily pursed lips and rosy cheeks which express Pleasure. Her eyes, however, are skewed sideways with fear of detection. Still, she seems literally bursting with glee, and her Flying Nun's coronet is doing likewise.

Which brings us to the unachievable Celibacy. On further reading in Wikipedia, we learn that in ancient Greece the apple was sacred to Aphrodite, the goddess of Love; and everyone knows, of course, about the forbidden fruit in the Garden of Eden, and the objectionable conduct Adam and Eve engaged in once they bit into it.... Thus the opening question—What has a nun to do with apples? And she is not just eating *one* apple—they are falling all around her. The plot thickens when we reflect on a drawn blue curtain behind her, because from Renaissance onward, artists often used such curtains to screen a bed.

Speak of the Devil... Let us consider another Botero image—that of Aphrodite, or Venus, as the painter calls her after the Roman fashion. What do you know!— it is the Nun's room, but with the curtain on the other side, which means this is the bed behind the Nun's curtain, and whatever our Nun is called here (be it Venus or Aphrodite), it is clearly the same woman—clothes are gone, but the apple remains, as is the rotundity of her pleasant form. This must have been the interval just before she positioned herself on the other side of the curtain, fully dressed and bursting with glee, as shown in the first image, and whatever it was she was doing in this interval, she clearly didn't have time enough to finish the apple.

Let us now consider when she would have time for the immodesty displayed in the second image. Traditional daily schedule in an average convent was as follows: Compline service rang in around 7:00 pm when everyone retired; Matins bells woke everyone around 4:00 am for prayer, then rest again; Prime service at 6:00 am, and the daily routine began all over. There were nine hours between

Compline and Matins, but only four between Matins and Prime. Bearing in mind that this sort of thing was probably done in the dead of night, we are, in all probability, seeing our Nun while Prime bells are ringing and the sun is rising behind the small dim window pane, which is presently attracting her attention. She is still in a dreamy never-never land, a kind of earthly eternity, watching her happiness whistle away with the night. There is no time to lose though—directly she must jump, dress, hide the shoes, hide the head band, hide the earrings and the watch (she has already hidden her companion either in the folds of the curtain or under the bed), take off her make-up, take off her red nail polish, open the window to get rid of the smell of the nail polish remover, grab the Bible and pretend total innocence, while fearfully but gleefully staring back at the curtain and, in her imagination, seeing apples fall around her, as in the first image.

And now about this Bible, to which she is holding on for dear life. It is bound in red. Why? Is it to distract from the leftover red nail polish stuck under cuticles, which she had managed to remove completely from her right hand, but not so completely from her left? And is it the Old Testament or the New? Because the Old Testament *instructs* in sin (it is known as 'Biblical Knowledge'), and the New Testament *discourages* it. Needless to say, should the Red Book combine both, the Old Testament and the New, our poor Nun is in a quandary; although, considering her own presently acquired (or perfected) Biblical Knowledge, she must certainly prefer the

Old Testament. In the next article, I should delve at length into the life of medieval nuns; and monks too. Literally *God only* knew what happened when they came together at confessionals and such, and apples began to fall from the sky... Can there be a doubt that they followed in the objectionable steps of Adam and Eve? Should anyone like a sneak preview, here is a wonderful 16th century painting by Cornelis Cornelz van Haarlem *A Monk at Confession* from the Frans Hals Museum in Haarlem, Holland.

Few maidens with any sizeable income remained unclaimed (i.e. unmarried) back in the Age Medieval. Certainly the income was always claimed. If it were deemed insufficient by mortal men, there was always the polygamous Lord in Heaven, who could afford to be less fastidious, and off to a monastery a girl went, having paid the necessary and sizable entry fee to join the army of Christ's brides. Because they lived in close quarters and shared communal life, the girls were called "sisters." A bridal ring was placed on their finger, however, lest their wedded state be called into question. Many of them, though, never having been introduced to the Lord in person, loved him very little, and as the saying goes, "marriage without love means love without marriage."

In the nearby monasteries lived and fussed 'brothers,' ever ready to question 'sisters'' wedded state. These European ecclesiastics, unlike their Egyptian precursors of the fourth century, did not lead a solitary ascetic life of the deserts, lying in the sand burnt by the sun and eating a couple of dry cicadas a day. Even the best of them were seldom able to school themselves into mere passive receptacles of the Holy Ghost. They therefore often presumed on religious familiarity to introduce themselves to their fair neighbors. Brothers and sisters invariably found solace from solitude in each other's company. What are relatives for.

After all, it wasn't so different from the early twentieth century—the days of men's and women's colleges—when Harvard came to visit Radcliff, Yale brought

 flowers to Connecticut College, or Columbia knocked on Barnard's doors.

It cannot surprise anyone that similar visits would result in still another Botero's image, where the mother gives the boy... an apple. But, in Scheherazade's fashion, more on the topic in the next article.

On Temptation: Is he from Heaven or is he from Hell/ This deep-ingressing Gabriel?

Although this article can be read independently, it is a continuation, in a sense, of the previous piece, which opened up the discussion concerning the servants of Christ, whether male or female, and their activities outside the boundaries of devotion.

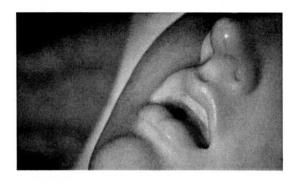

Let us now take a closer look at a young novice in a convent; chances are she is past-pubescent, anywhere between fifteen and early twenties. She would have left family and friends behind, and now finds herself under the celestial protection of the Madonna and her Divine Son; and, on a more earthly and intimate level, of the cold and exacting Mother Superior and perhaps a somewhat more sympathetic (depending on her degree of prettiness) Father Confessor. Her companions are other impressionable girls her age. She is compelled, by the rigors of convent life, and by the rules of monastic enclosure, to see little of men. Other than the aforementioned father confessor, additional male personages in her sphere—from a local provost and sundry clerics, to the Pope in Rome—are by degrees remote and aloof. Still, she reads much about this alarming gender in the Scriptures, which is her principal source of information on all things human and divine; and she also learns about it from the lives of saints—another required reading.

To be sure, all this material is full of misbehaving men—misbehaving towards women, naturally, with an occasional aberration to homosexuality. Our innocent novice undoubtedly discusses this fascinating and newly acquired wisdom with her young companions, and together they are at liberty to select Biblical passages that may answer their questions, but that are often more stimulating than elevating, particularly the Old Testament ones that initiate them in Biblical Knowledge, as demonstrated in the previous article. She is therefore encouraged, by her superiors, to prefer the New Testament to the Old, and it is from the New Testament that most homilies are delivered during services. They are delivered by men, because women, for reason of their lesser standing and inferior intellect, may not be heard in church, according to the all-knowing St. Paul. But curiosity kills the cat and corrupts a nun, and the Old Testament, with its titillating and mouth-watering stories, is not to be resisted. Surely the *Song of Songs* was read over and over again.

A brief diversion on the topic of proscribed literature: When I was growing up (in a country where any discussion of carnal pleasures was absolutely taboo), my family had a decent private library, but due to my young age, I was forbidden certain books. They were not locked away, though, since there was a tacit understanding that my parents could trust me not to do something they disapproved of, and on the whole I justified their trust. But not where illicit reading was concerned. I remember feeling horribly guilty as I lay at night, age 13 or about, hiding under the covers with a volume of unabridged *One Thousand and One Nights* and a flash light, reading about sheiks' "cannon shooting" between bed sheets perfumed with myrrh and frankincense in a mystically fragrant harem—the hot house of sensuality—where magical smoke softly billowed as it rose from smoldering embers in priceless vessels. Sheiks' activities were guarded by eunuchs whose 'cannon', alas, had been either disabled or removed altogether, but who dressed in exotic getups and stood at the ready behind the door, a curved scimitar stuck behind their silk belts ready to chop off an intruder's head. All the particulars were described in stirring detail—all the more stirring for the tasteful usage of perfumed allegory. From what I can remember of my impressions from that time, sheiks' ecstasies during 'cannon shooting' episodes were depicted with far greater precision than those of their concubines. Which, I suppose, is not surprising, considering that female circumcision has been practiced in the near east since time immemorial, rendering test subjects ecstasy-free.

Mercifully, western males had not come up with anything like this charming practice as regards their women. Even St. Paul, for all his misogyny, did not go that far. Silence them—yes; scorn them—certainly; beat them as often as they deserve—definitely; but not the unmentionable thing. Which means that our nuns' imagination, stirred by their post-pubescent physiology and Biblical enlightenment, was left to run wild.

If you are a woman reading this scribble, and if you happened to have lived in dormitories with other women (either at a boarding school, or in college), you may have observed that a while after moving in at the beginning of term, many girls began having their monthly periods at approximately the same time (it was certainly my experience, although I don't know whether there is a scientific explanation for this phenomenon). It is then safe to assume that however many centuries ago our neophytes lived and thrived, this must have been their experience as well. Now envision a group of young women, all thrown together behind thick stone walls, compliments of the Lord in Heaven who is presumed to love them all collectively with a husband's devotion. They are undernourished (Botero's nun is an exception), cold and forlorn in their shared cramps (some very severe), finding solace in each other's company, their imagination fueled by various very stirring devotional reading.

In addition to the Bible (both the Old Testament and the New), their immediate role models, who also suffered untold physical pains for the love of Christ, were the stars of the Christian pantheon—female saints of yore—of whom there was no dearth of written material to excite young and impressionable minds. There were all sorts of these women—a *smörgåsbord* of them—for every taste. Some had been married and went through childbirth before they became saints, some were ravished by objectionable males and then became saints (very imaginatively ravished, I may add, to qualify for the honor), some wished to be ravished, but also wished to resist the ravishing, embarking on various physical sufferings, which earned them martyrdom. As a sub-clause of the latter category, there was a whole genre of young women who so wished to be ravished, and so wished to resist it, that they dressed as men to earn admission to male monasteries as monks. I'd like to know how that worked, since there was absolutely no privacy in these monasteries (privacy is a modern luxury), and baths and latrines were all communal. Should anyone fall ill, a monk herbalist would visit them to examine their ailing bodies; and how, on earth, did these women hide their periods with no "feminine hygiene" paraphernalia (also a modern invention), and all that not counting plain human intuition of the men around them.

There is a monastery still in existence today, Mount Athos in north-eastern Greece, where women are categorically forbidden to enter, but where women dressed as men have always attempted to enter, but were presently apprehended and dealt with. Records are silent on what exactly these dealings consisted of, whether on Mount Athos or elsewhere, and whether today or in times of yore. They are not so silent on the goings on of monks, priests, and friars, though, who have, through history, been the worst violators of female chastity; and while it is undeniable that their advances were often virtuously resisted, it is equally true that that was not always the case.

Virtuous resistance (or should we say virtual), however, manifested itself in fantastical behavior now and again. As there was no lack of literary inspiration for the young women who found themselves buried within the tall stone walls of a convent, with only a library of "sacred" texts for consolation, their imaginings ran the visionary gamut, on occasion compelling them to try for the honor of sainthood and/or martyrdom, as did their predecessors. Take one such young woman, St. Teresa of Avila, who was deeply inspired by the passions of the female saints she had read about. As it was difficult for saints to represent spiritual love without recourse to physical love, and as there was not a single male representative among our Teresa's immediate acquaintance good enough to provide appropriate sensations, she had decided to become a *true* bride of Christ. In a great show of appreciation, the obliging deity had presently dispatched an angel for suitable ingress, not unlike God the Father dispatching Archangel Gabriel to impregnate Mary fifteen hundred years earlier. In Mary's case, the great event is known as the Annunciation (on which one may read further in the *Annunciation* article). Both God the Father and God the Son seemed to prefer delegating these functions to messenger angels, unlike pagan gods who preceded them, and who would much rather do this agreeable sort of thing themselves.

Our Teresa, although fifteen centuries younger than Mary, was not to be outdone. Her case became known as the Mystical Piercing by The Spear of Divine Love. Apocryphally, it was her heart that was mystically pierced. But if one examines Bernini's take on the event, called Ecstasy of St. Teresa, which compelling sculpture one may admire in Santa Maria della Vittoria, Rome, one shall see that the piercing may not have been  very mystical; that The Spear of Divine Love may be aiming somewhat lower than the heart; that the angel is having much too good a time; and that the limbs of the future saint, although covered in voluminous textile, thrash about underneath this textile with all the conviction of earthly, rather than heavenly, ecstasy. The generous lady clearly allowed much room for interpretation in the account of her experiences that she left behind, both in her autobiography, called *Life of Teresa of Jesus*, and in her other seminal work, *The Interior Castle*. Both are an integral part of Christian mysticism and Christian meditation practices. She was canonized forty years after her death. Few things in this life, or in the next one, equal self-promotion.

This obviously is not the place for a comprehensive dissertation on female saints, but just one more example might be suitable—that of St. Catherine of Siena. This one was not satisfied with messenger boys, and wished for direct Divine familiarity. The Lord obliged, and appeared to her as a handsome young man with long hair and a long red robe, bidding her to lie on her back. He then invited her to expose herself, rolled up his sleeve and tore the heart out of her body, causing her the most marvelous surge of pain. She lived without the heart a couple of days, missing Him terribly, but, in his Divine benevolence, he eventually reappeared and placed his own much larger organ inside her to replace the one she was missing. The exchange of hearts was followed by an exchange of invisible rings, and they were wed. She later claimed that the ring she wore was a mystical replica of her divine husband's foreskin (born Jewish, he was circumcised)—the only part of physical Jesus that certainly remained on Earth.

No wonder Catherine claimed it for herself, since this part of Christ's original equipment was the most prized relic of all in an age when relics were valued above all else. It was believed that Mary had carried it on her person, near her heart, till she died. More than a dozen churches, including Saint John Lateran, the Pope's church, claimed to own a piece of Holy Foreskin. One female saint, who also claimed to have possessed a segment, maintained she swallowed it at communion. (One can only wonder what happened to it after this ingestion). John Calvin, to give him credit, was dubious that such a small bit of epidermis could be so often divided. Still, at one abbey church in France, their own fragment was thought to cure sterility in women and insure painless delivery. In the early fifteenth century, Queen Catherine of England borrowed it for that purpose, and so happy was she and her husband (Henry V) with the result (future Henry VI), that they gave the abbey funds to build a special sanctuary to hold it, once they returned it. We'll never know what exactly she did with it to make it work while it was in her possession.

▼

And here we have it. Not only the carefully recorded lives of numerous female saints were available to our young novices for their agitated perusal and fantasy, but all the particulars of Jesus' own life (including his anatomical particulars) were there to contemplate and have visions about. Ah, those visions... The great difficulty was to decide whether they were sent by God or Satan, for Satan is sly and can disguise himself as an angel to lead a young woman astray. Not that some young women minded terribly such going astray... But as their male counterparts knew back then (many still do), women did not have the reasoning powers of men; they were the "weaker vessel," whose limited mental capacities, unbridled curiosity (always that apple) and insatiable lusts made them easy prey to the devil's snares.

Little wonder that these propensities proved an endless inspiration for artists, who became professional visualizers of saintly stories. These artists gave outward form to the dreams of the devout, and their function was to encourage the pious and stimulate them further in their devotions—of which more anon.

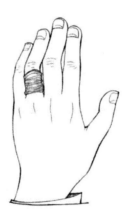

Annunciation vs. Violation vs. Insemination

This is the third installment of the discourse begun with *Nun vs. Aphrodite* and developed further in *Temptation*. It is the discourse on nuns, angels, saints, monks, priests, and other sundry religious personalities and their activities vis-à-vis each other while ever mindful of God the Father, the Son, and the Holy Ghost. Again, the other two and this one can be read separately or in conjunction with others.

As before, I shall be doing this with pictorial assistance. As Alice famously and justly exclaimed, "what good is a book without pictures," I take the liberty to extend her sentiment to all writing. Most certainly the writing on matters spiritual, for it was the artists' marvelous skills that made them such handy interpreters of an exotic saintly language into a more familiar human tongue. (*Nota bene* from Wikipedia: *exotic* is not to be confused with *erotic*. While the former signifies being, or characteristic of, a strange or unusual place, the latter means giving sexual pleasure or sexually arousing). But Wikipedia was not available at the time when artists translated Saintly into Human, and therefore we cannot blame our nuns for confusing the two words, and consequently for misunderstanding the artists' interpretations sometimes.

▼

There was once a young nun (let us call her Celestina) living a rather exhilarating life in a quiet convent among the scenic northern hills of sixteenth century Italy. Celestina, who left a memoir, was often visited in her cell by St. Catherine of Siena, the one with an invisible replica of Christ's foreskin for a wedding ring. "St. Catherine," wrote Celestina, "was dressed

just as one sees her in paintings." Because this particular convent was not fully enclosed ('fully enclosed' meant no one went in or out—a veritable tomb; most convents were not so unreasonable), Celestina could see such paintings in the parish church, or in other churches in the area where she and her soul mates attended Mass and received the sacraments.

The majority of the European population outside convents and monasteries couldn't read, and a priest who recited biblical passages from his pulpit recited them in Latin, which the congregation did not understand, and often the priest didn't either. Biblical content was therefore learned from pictures, not unlike pre-schoolers today who learn from picture books. In other words, pictures were the Bible for the illiterate—whether stained glass windows in the north, or frescoed walls in the south. All the most important episodes from the Old and the New Testaments were carefully and variously depicted for the benefit of the devout, and every place of worship was so decorated. Among these episodes, few biblical events captured popular imagination as forcibly as the *Annunciation*, or proved as provoking and titillating to artists (and almost certainly to nuns).

Allow me to explain the term "annunciation" to those who may not be familiar with it. Because God the Father, in order to become a father, preferred to delegate his duties to messenger boys, he sent the Archangel Gabriel to act on his behalf as regards Mary. As much as he may have wished to break with tradition this time and do whatever was needed himself, it clearly couldn't be done without losing his standing in the celestial hierarchy. Yet I can't imagine him not wishing to break with tradition this one time. He singled this wisp of a girl out of all other fourteen-year-olds, and considering that his options were as limitless as the heavens that held Him, he must have liked her prodigiously. The intensity of His sacrifice must be greatly appreciated by all the devout. According to the Christian tenet, Mary became pregnant with Jesus the moment Gabriel's words to her, "Behold the maiden shall conceive," entered her ears. Indeed, for the longest time female ears were painted resolutely covered (with hair, or veil, or cap), because they were viewed on par with sexual organs as a result of this momentous annunciation by Gabriel; or rather because of its outcome. Not till Renaissance were the ears allowed to come out of hiding. Since Gabriel actually borrowed his prophetic phrase from Isaiah 7:14, Mary was often shown in *Annunciation* paintings with a volume of the Old Testament, reading Isaiah's pronouncement when Gabriel showed up and decided to be redundant.

According to apocryphal tradition, Mary was a Temple virgin—one among several—when the High Priest decided that those Temple virgins who had reached age fourteen should be made useful, whereupon young men, and not so young, were invited to come around and claim them as property. In Mary's case however, on account of her exceptional loveliness, so many turned up, eager to call her their own, that a contest had to be organized. Each suitor was invited to bring a wooden rod, and whichever of these rods should bloom, its owner was the winner. The possibility that several rods might have bloomed at once was never entertained by the tradition, and sure enough, only one did. Why the elderly Joseph's rod should have bloomed, while the rods of much younger and more vigorous men did not, is anyone's guess, but Joseph became the chosen one. Chosen under one condition—that after the wedding Mary was still to remain under the Temple protection awhile in her virginal state. It was then that Gabriel beat Joseph to it and impregnated his wife by whispering sweet nothings into her ear. It appears Joseph was chosen to become the most famous cuckold in history. What makes it even better, is that once Joseph was acquainted with the particulars of the winged visit, he rejoiced at the news. He was professedly happy for his wife's sake. Where—oh—where are such husbands to be found!

It made sense therefore that as art developed during the early Renaissance, and artists learned how to depict convincing-looking people inside convincing-looking spaces, doing convincing-looking things, it became fashionable to place a convincing-looking Mary inside a convincing-looking bedroom during Gabriel's very convincing-looking annunciation.

Let us now look at the early 16th century variation on the theme by Lorenzo Lotto—something of the sort our Celestina would have seen in local churches. Lotto, a child of Renaissance, had employed all the developments that had taken place in painting techniques in the preceding hundred years—perspective, foreshortening, modeling, movement, emotional depiction—in short, all the tricks of trade available to him to achieve 'naturalism,' or, in other words, to achieve the best possible translation from Saintly to Human.

There could be no doubt as to how Lotto interpreted the incident: a mixed blessing in blessed disguise.

There, for all to see, is God the Father, torpedoing out of the clouds, his divine body language autocratically declaring—"Get her!" There is the beauteous messenger with a lily in his left hand, his right hand raised in self-righteous indignation—"Don't you know what's good for you! Can't you see *we* brought you *flowers!*" And then there is the poor kitty that probably a moment ago sat purring on the girl's lap as she stroked his soft fur, but went tumbling down as the girl jumped in fright at the startling  assault, and was now hissing in panic at the trespasser. Surely there is no better indicator of any given circumstance than an animal instinct. And finally there is the girl herself, age fourteen, wrenched out of her quiet revelry as she sat peacefully and unsuspectingly in her bedroom, her kitty on her lap, contentedly reading Isaiah and contemplating a fetching Italian landscape. Now, in desperation —because the way out was decisively cut off to her—she ran to the opposite wall (that opened to the hapless observer), her dress still billowing, to beg for help!

What was our Celestina to think as she gazed at such a painting, as helpless to help Mary, as Mary was to oppose the intruders! She was probably not much older than Mary had been, and powers of association are persuasive indeed, particularly under the influence of a convincing work of art that in itself appears divine. And who knows the degree of importance that a young, impressionable and inexperienced girl might attach to a similar apparition. She may reasonably well have thought that Gabriel was quite good looking, and so much resembling the young Father Angelo, who had recently replaced the old and ugly father confessor just gone off to a better life, God bless his soul and keep it safe. And here was the bed, and the kitty, and it could all be so comfortable and cozy, if only God the Father didn't choose *to watch*, and the angel had given a bit of an advance notice rather than appearing so suddenly and unexpectedly. Mary may even have liked it. And should she, Celestina, reveal her thoughts to the handsome newcomer at the confession? It would be a sin not to do so, but would she not be endangering her soul even more by admitting her thoughts to him rather than hiding them? Because she couldn't help noticing that Father Angelo did not look at her with the same indifferent benevolence as did his predecessor...

Such is the miracle of great art. Such is *Annunciation*. A wolf in sheep's clothing? A ravager in angel's cloak?

But one may object that Celestina lived in the sixteenth century, with all the benefits of "modern technology" (read "advanced painting techniques") that made *Annunciation* as vivid to her as if she sat in a New York movie theater today watching the action unfold. How was the same scene conveyed three hundred years earlier, before advances in figurative art made biblical narratives graphically corporeal? Let us travel north to Reims, France, geographically, and in time back to the thirteen century. Reims's builders were just finishing the construction of their city's glorious new Gothic cathedral, and the sculptors were taking over with stone-carved biblical narratives, *Annunciation* among them. They placed *Annunciation* a little above eye level on the splayed outer wall to the left of the main entrance—easy to see for anyone coming in or going out.

This one is very economical in design. Just the two solitary figures—Mary and Gabriel—meeting each other on the cathedral facade. No bedroom, no bed, no kitty, no book, no lily—no superfluous paraphernalia of any sort, and that includes (or rather excludes) God the Father. This particular Mary isn't frightened, nor does she protest, but appears obediently resigned to her fate. This is not surprising, for the leading theologian of the day, who informed all humanity with his wisdom, Doctor Thomas Aquinas, following Aristotelian tenet, proclaimed women to be passive receptacles of the active male seed, serving as no more than an incubator for the developing fetus. No doubt Reims sculptors, instructed by the cathedral's theologians, were obliged to follow the prevailing dogma and portray Mary accordingly. Still, too bad her hands have gone missing over time, because hands are expressive, and these hands could have conceivably conveyed covert meaning disallowed to the rest of her body by the orthodoxy of the time. Her very young age is hinted at by the small youthful breasts protruding through her tunic. Nothing remarkable about her person otherwise.

Not so Gabriel the Charmer. Mary may be compliant and apathetic *à la* Aquinas, but the good Doctor imposed no restrictions on men (or on angels), and our archangel is having the best of times. Never mind she is irresponsive while he is nudging her forward with his remaining wing. He is God's messenger and a one man act. His grin is as irresistible as it is naughty. It goes perfectly with the gesture of his left hand, which has mercifully survived through time, unlike Mary's hands and his own right hand which may have held a lily. Even the pointing finger survived! And where is it pointing? Why, it's pointing to whatever stirs behind the lifted hem of his cape.

He is supposed to be saying "Behold a maiden shall conceive!" But it looks for all the world that his actual words are: "Look what I've got for you... Would you like me to drop the hem? That should cheer you up!"

A fascinating thing about this teasing Gabriel is that his original head (like his right wing and his right hand) had been lost and was replaced at an uncertain date with a  head from another statue. Do observe that it is too small for his body. (Mary is much more in proportion, if not in spirit).

But what this means is that whoever was in charge of finding an appropriate head to replace the lost original, did not worry nearly as much about proportions as they did about *a facial expression* they felt should match *the finger's gesture.* That gesture birthed two birds with one stone finger—not only did it point Mary in the right direction, it also pointed restorers in the right direction of the original sculptor's mind. That thirteenth-century craftsman who carved the statue in the first place was a brilliant interpreter of Saintly into Human. For such indeed was his understanding of human sentiment, that his masterpiece continued to hit human nerve even when its pieces went missing (a head no less)! Europe had not seen such ability since classical Greece ceased to exist two millennia earlier.

But if an unknown restorer felt the movement of the finger, so did others to be sure. In an age before print, and before a wide distribution of books, one was much more attuned to imagery than one is today, and felt it as profoundly as we feel a written word or an image on a movie screen. And if among those others there were a very young woman, and a young woman destined for celibacy, whether a sixteenth-century Celestina gazing at a Lotto in Italy, or a thirteenth century Celeste walking through Reims' central portal in France, the true meaning of *Annunciation* could not have escaped her, and her young dreams back in her cold convent cell could not have been peaceful.

And if this very young woman were a student of art history today, and her learning unlocked the doors to the past and opened her eyes to what Celestina/Celeste may have truly felt while gazing at their respective *Annunciations,* she, while gazing at a similar painting herself, could surely envision herself in Mary's place, as a fourteen year old, reading quietly in her room while the others were away. Suddenly the door should be thrown open and a perfect stranger should come in with wings attached to his back (and it wouldn't even be Halloween), and he would smile, and come closer, and tell her she shall have a beautiful baby.

In any western democracy today this stranger would be behind bars on charges of statutory misbehavior. Yet glorious *Annunciations* are worshipped around the world with untiring devotion. Art is indeed a thing of wonder.

On Naughty Habits, Gods of Yore, and Kellogg Flakes

This is a stand-alone scribble that was inspired by a curious piece of information I incidentally came upon, having to do with Kellogg Flakes and Graham Crackers, which were invented, it turned out, with the purpose of discouraging boys from masturbation. The thing was irresistible.

▼

In the beginning was Atum.

He was Egypt's first god, and his origin is a mystery. It was a

mystery to him too, for there was no one else to be mystified. By the time he became conscious of himself, he was further perplexed whether he had appeared a full grown man or a babe, for so long was his development that its beginnings were lost in time and in mind. His behavior was not a mystery, however. All alone, with no one to love and cherish, and with only his own body for a solitary companion, he loved and cherished his own body. Indeed, who can ever be dearer to oneself, than oneself? This affection was all the more extraordinary because it was entirely disinterested. His right hand (judging by the imagery, Atum was right-handed) became his only friend, his sister, and his spouse. He called her Iusaaset (the great one who glides forth) and she became a goddess in her own right. It was with warmth, firmness and energy that Iusaaset and Atum loved Atum. Enthusiastic, they were groping in the dark, so to speak, for friendless and innocent of all knowledge, they had no idea of their prowess. From their energy, matter immerged. Millennia later, in a different country, under different circumstances, a famous scientist—godlike himself in his powers of deduction—would express this concept in a mass-energy equivalence formula: $E = mc^2$ asserting that mass is a property of all energy, and energy is a property of all mass.

Meanwhile, unaware of the future and its scientist, Iusaaset and Atum carried on, and out of the energy they generated, a mass of seed materialized that contained more energy still, and once that seed fell upon the fertile soil of Egypt, more mass emerged, this time of Egyptian gods and Egyptian inhabitants. The inhabitants, alert to the fact that they owed their existence to Iusaaset and Atum's activities, soon equated these activities with those of the Nile, the great river that assured their continuous existence. The Nile's ebb and flow were seen by them as an expression of the frequency with which Iusaaset glided forth upon Atum. Said inhabitants then compelled their pharaohs, the living manifestations of gods on earth, to do the same: in well-attended (and well-recorded) ceremonies, a ruling pharaoh was expected to activate his own Iusaaset upon his own Atum, with the proceeds spilled into the river to assure its unremitting ebbing and flowing. Atum be blessed. So much for Egypt.

In the interim, to the north-east of Egypt, in ancient Sumeria, as primordial as Egypt itself, and situated between the Tigris and Euphrates rivers, the lore evolved along similar lines. Creative Force may have different names in different languages, but it remains creative force. Egyptian Atum was Sumerian Enki. And Enki employed the same extremity in his creative process as did Atum. The only difference is that no Right Hand, or any hand, is recorded to have proffered assistance, which doesn't mean the hand wasn't there; only that it was of secondary importance and not worthy of recording. Throughout history, alas, much honest credit has never been given where credit was due. The recipe for Enki's creation of the first human is as follows.

Ingredients:
   3 parts all-purpose Tigris mud (could be substituted with that of Euphrates)
   1 part all-purpose water (from either river)
   ¼ part salt water from the Red Sea
   ½ part all-purpose mountain goat milk (the milk is all-purpose, not the goat)
   2 parts self-generated self-rising seed

Directions:
1. Combine mud, water and salt water in a large wooden bowl and mix thoroughly, otherwise mud will lump when seed is added. Self-generate 1 part of the required

seed and slowly, very slowly, stir into the mixture till fully blended. Cover loosely and let stand until bubbly. Leave thus covered at air temperature. Consider this day 1 of the 10 day cycle.

2. Day 2: Stir mixture with whatever is at hand. Wait for it to thicken. (Here the historical record is ambiguous—is it the mixture that should thicken or the stirrer? Both, presumably, for better efficiency).

3. Day 3: look at yourself in a nearby lake and mold the clay in your own image to the best of your abilities.

4. Day 4: let the clay figure dry in a shade to prevent cracking.

5. Day 5: pour some of the goat milk into the figure's mouth. The figure should come alive and begin to complain of solitude. Call it Man.

6. Day 6: observe all the deficiencies which should become apparent once Man is in action, and with those in mind spend days 7 through 9 in molding an improved model; you may engage Man's assistance with seed-generation. Call the superior product Woman.

7. Retire on day 10 and observe the two interact. They should take care of further creation.

Enki be blessed. So much for Mesopotamia.

About a millennium after the Egyptian Atum and the Mesopotamian Enki did what they must, in a neighboring land, called Palestine, to the east of Sumeria, there appeared Jehovah, known to later generations as God of the Jews. Annoyed at not having been there first, and to make up for the "Jehovah-come-lately" effect, he invented a very clever concept of "transcendentalism" and applied it to himself, claiming to have existed *beyond* and *before* time, whether one noticed it or not. No one did in fact, for there was no one to notice at the time. (Atum and Enki, and their people, knowing the truth, treated these claims for the tall tales they were and ignored them altogether.) Jehovah was thus faced with the necessity to create another group of individuals who'd accept his declarations on faith, a freshly made group, inexperienced and gullible.

It is one thing, however, to decide upon a completely new course of action, and quite another to implement it. The easiest thing in such instances is to put into practice the working models already in existence. In Jehovah's case they were the Egyptian and Sumerian models. But which to choose? After considering the relative merits of each, Jehovah seems to have decided to try both. The reason for our own uncertainly vis-à-vis his choice is that by the time his actions were recorded by Man many thousands of years later, they were apparently mixed up and distorted, Man being imperfect, which is why the Bible provides two conflicting accounts of Jehovah's activities and shortens the number of days of creation from ten to seven in both accounts.

In the first one (Gen. I: 27-28), Jehovah created man and woman simultaneously, in his own image, which suggests his own androgynous nature. In this type of creation he must have followed the model of Atum the Egyptian, which involved the use of the Right Hand, although no particulars are given. According to the second account, Jehovah clearly followed the model of Enki the Sumerian, creating Man first (Gen. II: 7) and then Woman (Gen. II: 22). Except unlike the Sumerian original, in the Hebrew Bible

111

version, Woman is manufactured out of Man's rib. *But what has **a rib** to do with creation?* It certainly does not generate seed, as per Enki's recipe, rendering it useless. Since it is difficult to imagine that a god (however late he may have come on the scene and however unskillful therewith) should not be able to follow another god's recipe—and surely Jehovah followed Enki's prescription fastidiously—it must have been the scribes who got things wrong as they wrote down the primordial deed many hundreds of years later. They based their information, naturally, on the oral tradition that was narrated from generation to generation, altered and embroidered with human fantasy through the ages.

Think of an ancient mother telling a bed-time creation story to her child before the child went to sleep at night. Obviously she wouldn't tell *the real thing* for fear that the child might have a nightmare, scream in the night, and wake up the household, not to mention rouse the neighbors, who should certainly inquire into the nature of the child's distress. And *what would the neighbors say* when told the truth?! Thus *the real thing* got replaced with *a rib.*

Sure enough, a cursory scholarship reveals that *rib* and *penis* were designated by the same, or nearly the same, word in Enki's Sumerian; sort of like the word *extremity* in English means a variety of things. Consider the possibilities of misinterpretation and mistranslation: in addition to "disaster," "excess," and "frontier," *extremity* can also mean *any* projecting member of a human body. Indeed, a characteristic feature of Sumerian was the large number of homophones (words with the same structure but different meanings), in addition to the bewildering amount and variety of phonetic values that identical signs could have.

Both these phenomena would certainly lead to a deviation in translating the Sumerian into another language—Hebrew, for instance. We can thus pretty safely posit that *a rib* had little to do with creating anything, least of all Woman, and revert to the *extremity* that really mattered.

In this, however, there is a further dilemma with the Biblical accounts as they came down to us, in that Jehovah instructed Man and Woman to be fruitful (Gen. I: 28), yet he not only didn't teach them how to go about it, but worse still—forbid them to learn by themselves. They could neither learn through tasting of the fruit of knowledge, nor were they allowed to talk to the well-informed Serpent. How did Jehovah expect them to follow his bidding? Since the Bible is again silent on the subject, the only logical conclusion is that Man was encouraged to follow the Atum/Enki model of self-germination through self-stimulation (which doesn't need to be learned because innately grasped), with Woman's task left uncertain. Perhaps hers was the role of the Right Hand, or, alternatively, perhaps she was meant to help in raising the off-spring, or both. But either or both—it was left for her to figure out.

Which, in the first recorded act of civil disobedience, she did—by defying her creator. She did converse with the erudite reptile, and did taste of the fruit of knowledge, and did encourage Man to follow her example. Man and Woman thus learned what to do with one another. They were consequently expelled by Jehovah from his horticultural patch into the desert to fare for themselves, which they did with surprising skill, putting their freshly-acquired knowledge to the test upon the soft turf of the very first oasis they chanced to encounter. With time, they passed on this skill to succeeding generations, and much progeny was engendered in the following centuries by their brood, and their brood's brood. So much, indeed, that with time their numbers were deemed respectable enough by the exacting deity to return to them his favor and, more to the point, to proclaim them his chosen people, even if no other gods considered them so, which was other gods' loss to be sure.

There was a price to pay for being "chosen" though. The price of the god's benevolence was his subjects' foreskins. Jehovah's reasoning was logical, if vindictive. "Well, fine," he seems to have said, "you've learned of the forbidden fruit despite my express prohibition. So be it. But then never mind using it for anything but procreation. Which means NO IDLE RECREATION! In fact, you naughty children, to make sure you don't fuss with your *extremity* unproductively, give me back *the flabby fringe,* so you have nothing to hold on to." The ancient recreation was now deemed divine privilege only, sanctioned by original creation, and Man's engagement in it proclaimed sacrilegious and discouraged through the removal of his play-worthy prepuce.

They were a devout lot indeed, those who abided by Jehovah's extraordinary prohibition and embraced the painful procedure. But still more surprising are those who turned their backs on Jehovah in later centuries, preferring his Son instead (who kindly allowed them to keep their prepuces), but who continued to deny themselves self-stimulation, despite the Son's having said nothing at all against a little idle recreation, understanding and compassionate as he was. The likes of Titus Flavius Clemens, for example, known to posterity as Clement of Alexandria, the second century Christian theologian, *would* express his horror of spilling seed: "... the seed is not to be vainly ejaculated, nor is it to be damaged, nor is it to be wasted," and others concurred, having long lost sight of original reasons for similar prohibition, which no longer existed. The great St. Augustine of Hippo, who, as a young man, had gone to the outmost limits of depravity and back before his conversion to Christianity in the end of the fourth century, expressly and categorically forbid even the simplest of pleasures to later generations. St. Augustine must not have read his Bible very carefully, for all his learning, for had he done so, he would have remembered the Golden Rule: "don't do unto others what you shouldn't like to be done unto you." Instead, he replaced it with another Rule: "do as I say and not as I do."

A potent thing is Tradition. It takes possession of the mind more powerfully than any amount of reason or judgment ever can. It defines our characters and carries us through centuries. It is indelibly intertwined with faith, and multitudes bow to it without doubt or hesitation. Reason will be denounced before tradition condemned, and an inquiry into its causes is sacrilegious for it might contradict its own tenets by exposing the origins that have nothing to do with subsequent uses. Such has certainly proved to be the Judeo-Christian tradition, which, having recycled and tweaked earlier beliefs, succeeded entirely in superseding them. Both Atum and Enki were neglected and forgotten, while Jehovah and his creed became indeed transcendental.

It is thus, across centuries of tradition, that we arrive at the eighteenth century, otherwise known as the Age of

Enlightenment. Back to the obliging Wikipedia, where the first line on the subject reads: Age of Enlightenment (or Age of Reason) was a cultural movement of intellectuals in 18th century Europe and the United States, whose purpose was to reform society and advance knowledge. It promoted science and intellectual interchange and opposed superstition, intolerance and abuses by church and state..." This may be, and yet the aforementioned intellectuals held on to at least one bit of intolerance from the intolerable past—nay, made the harmless little auto-eroticism more intolerable still. The question is *why*? What did they do in-between "reforming society and advancing knowledge"? Was knowledge *all* they were advancing? Might they not have also been advancing St. Augustine's method of "do as I say and not as I do?"

Did they feel pangs of guilt thereof? Because the fury they unleashed in the direction of "solitary vice" was unlike anything seen before. Even Jehovah couldn't compete. To be sure, Jehovah was removed from it altogether. Faithful in their devotion to their new god, Science, the enlightened intellectuals freed "the vice" from the shackles of religious condemnation. Only to wrap it in a mantle of scientific denunciation. In the name of Knowledge, they whipped phobia into a frenzy.

Learned treatises on the titillating subject began to appear in the early 1700's, but let us cut to the quick with the most influential of them all, written in 1760 by the Swiss physician of French origin, Samuel-Auguste Tissot. Called "*L'Onanisme*," it presented a comprehensive medical dissertation on the ill-effects of masturbation. The word "Onanism," otherwise known as "The Sin of Onan," needs to be explained first. In biblical times, under Jewish law, a brother was required to procreate with his deceased brother's widow. Onan of Judah refused to comply, and spilled his seed on the ground instead (Gen. 38). This is the origin of the term, which is in fact incorrectly used, for if one reads this Biblical passage with the mandatory piety and zeal, one realizes that what really happened was *coitus interruptus*. Dr. Tissot, who was French, not Jewish, may have read a mistranslated version of the Scriptures (recall the rib/penis mix-up); or else, as Prof. Higgins once said, "the French don't really care what they say, as long as they pronounce it properly." Whatever the case, the misnomer stuck.

In his seminal exposition, the good doctor argued that semen was an "essential oil" and "stimulus" which, when lost from the body in great amounts, would cause "a perceptible reduction of strength, of memory and even of reason; blurred vision, nervous disorders, all types of gout and rheumatism, weakening of the organs of generation, blood in the urine, disturbance of the appetite, headaches and a great number of other disorders." (In a similar vein, in the later-day United States, where everything was compared to finance, a man's body was regarded as a bank, and any unnecessary withdrawal of semen-capital was ill-advised, for that too would promote no end of ill fortune.) Where there is a leader with a sensational message, there'll always be followers. It makes no difference whether the message be sensible, so long as it is dramatic. Following in Dr. Tissot's illuminating steps, a stupefying number of prominent physicians, scientists, philosophers, and religious leaders proclaimed, with the deepest of beliefs, that illnesses such as insanity, vision and hearing problems, epilepsy, mental retardation, and general health problems were caused by self-stimulation. Over 60% of medical and mental illnesses were blamed on masturbation. The dread of it was so great that extreme preventative measures were instituted throughout. At first they consisted of mechanical restraints and physical discipline.

Here are half a dozen examples of mechanical devices that parents were urged to use on their male children, with explanations therewith. Needless to say, should one require visual demonstrations, which I decided to omit here for reasons of their hideousness, one can look them up.

1. Simple Bondage. Just tie up the young culprit so he can't touch himself, and spoon-feed him when hungry.

2. Spermatorrhea Bandage. Never mind tying him up whole—just keep the penis securely bound and make sure he can't unbind it, thus making it impossible to have an erection. Should he contrive to loosen the dressing, wallop him.

3. Leather-Jacket Corset. Here things got more sophisticated. A corset made of leather and steel was introduced in Europe in the 1830's. It included a metal penis tube with a steel band permanently riveted to the shield, which was attached to a boy's body in such a manner that it could not be removed, and thus prevented access to the testicles. Even the young Houdini could not have gotten his little houdini out of this thing.

4. The Stephenson Spermatic Truss came forty years later. This gadget placed the penis in a tight pouch stretched and tied down between the legs, which made erections impossible. The benevolent Mr. Stephenson was so good as to change his contraption slightly some twenty years

later. He did allow the penis to move freely, but added a metal hood with sharp spikes inside it. Should a boy be so lucky as to feel the delights of an impending erection, it would be presently driven against the spikes and safely foiled.

5. Bowen Device was like a cup. It was placed over the head of the penis and attached to pubic hair by chains and clips. When the wearer got an erection, the pubic hair would be plucked painfully, which resulted in its repression.

6. Sexual Armor was sort of a male chastity belt—a jacket with leather pants which supported a large piece of steel armor. Perforations in the armor allowed urine to escape, but the bolted, padlocked trapdoor at the rear would have to be opened by an independent bystander to allow for bowel movement.

The list goes on.

Nowhere was the panic so sweeping and wholesale as in the United States, and nowhere so resolute the determination to rid the country of the infection. Never, even in the midst of the most extreme phobia vis-à-vis self-stimulation, did Europe ever contemplate genital surgery. Sexual mutilation was the provenance of the followers of Jehovah, the objectionable Hebrews, with their millenarian Covenant, and having doggedly persecuted them for two thousand years, Europe was loath to embrace the *Jewish Rite*. Europeans figured that Jehovah's Divine Son had corrected the Father's mistakes, and it would be an abomination to contravene his corrections, which have become the hoary and venerated tradition in their own right. Such a cure would be far worse than the disease itself.

The United States, however, had no similar prejudices. A young country possessed of unlimited aspiration and dispossessed of inhibiting tradition, it combined innocence with impartiality and added extra zeal to whatever it undertook.

By the end of the 19th century, the very influential Dr. John Harvey Kellogg felt that masturbation destroyed not only one's physical and mental health, but moral health as well, and pronounced that "neither the plague, nor war, nor small-pox, nor similar diseases, have produced results so disastrous to humanity as the pernicious habit of onanism." Since a victim literally *died by his own hand*, the good doctor regarded it a form of suicide. Pronouncing sex for anything but reproduction purposes to be a shocking excess, Dr. Kellogg, like some latter-day Jehovah, urged routine circumcision as a deterrent to masturbation. And guess what? America clicked its heels and followed the leader. To this day, a great number of newborn boys (from Christian and agnostic families) are routinely circumcised at birth in our country, and the parents who authorize the procedure have little idea of the real reason behind it, which has been largely lost in the annals of history.

And was Dr. Kellogg content with his accomplishment? Never. No enthusiastic reformer anxious for the betterment of the world can ever be satisfied with minor accomplishments and rest on his laurels. Suppose some individuals are so congenitally wicked and corrupt, that even circumcision couldn't save them from themselves. What then? It was at this point that our doctor had a revelation that a major culprit in provoking the *urge* was *diet*. But of course! It's the spices, the sweets, the objectionable treats that warm the soul, stir the appetite and salivate the palate, stimulating other desires as well, far less innocent than appetite, that are at fault. Away with delicacies! Only the most tasteless and plainest of foods have the power to circumvent the outrageous impulse.

No sooner said than done, Kellogg Flakes were conceived, produced, and advertised as the blandest, non-stimulating, *pre-digested* alternative to food that all responsible parents must themselves ingest and feed to their young. And all parents did. Well, in the US they did. (No one can ever imagine the French so to forget their priorities as to start replacing their or their children's morning *croissant* and *café au lait* with Dr. Kellogg's mix, whatever *les hasards*.) Indeed, so successful and profitable was the new invention, that competition soon jumped into the fray. Up onto the pulpit climbed the stern and eager *Reverend Sylvester Graham, a box of Graham Crackers pressed fervently to the narrow chest, eyes raised in humble devotion, while reciting, in sonorous and resonant voice, the benefits of this latest gift to humanity—the one true manna fit for the diet of the devout Christian.*

And what of the congregation? Why, it was there to hear and obey of course. It is there still. Perhaps in larger numbers in supermarkets than in churches these days, which stands to reason for they must choose their crackers and cereals (of which the variety has increased a hundred-fold), but still placing their faith in the salutary advantages of these dietary staples. The pulpit has long been replaced by the TV screen, and the message itself may have changed beyond recognition, yet the power of advertisement never waivers. So supple is this power, so tenacious its ability to adjust to changed circumstances, that it has long reached distant shores—the lands far beyond those where the long-forgotten Atum once held forth with his Iusaaset, and where Enki stirred his brew.

To Atum and to Enki belonged millennia of glory, and then millennia of oblivion. But in oblivion their fortune was safe from all reverses and even their defeat may have acquired the splendor of victory. With their seed they fertilized the world. Forces of nature, they personified nature. Their very flaws (if flaws they be) were those of resemblance between god and man. Are they truly forgotten? Have they not proven to be as transcendental as any other god claiming this distinction? Might not the censorious latecomers have been *intransigent* rather than *transcendental*? Might there not be another case of a mistranslation? And might not human hands continue to glide upon the marble shafts of ancient columns—the noble remnants of fallen temples?

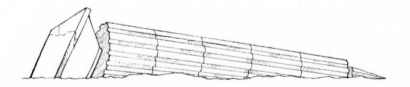

Intermezzo

Because the majority of the articles in this collection have been inspired by travelling and observation, it seems appropriate to conclude it with three short travelogues written after visiting three fascinating European locations, in three consecutive years, via three methods of transportation respectively—coach, rail and sail. These journeys were organized by a redoubtable scholastic institution located in Switzerland, where my husband was a dutiful student in his teen years many a decade back. Founded in the late 19th century on the British model, this was, and still remains, one of the oldest such establishments in Switzerland. A few words on the British model seem in order, as that may give the reader a better idea of the Swiss establishment and its denizens.

These venerable British institutions, which are still called, with a seemingly British sense of irony, public schools, had long been steeped in tradition by the time the Swiss school in question was founded, and, contrary to appearances, irony had nothing to do with their appellation. They emerged sometime in the Elizabethan England as charity schools meant to educate poor scholars. The idea of democracy, however, was a long way away, and the Elizabethan do-gooders who founded these schools on the old monastic model, used the term "public" simply to indicate that access to them was not restricted on the basis of religion, occupation, or home location. In other words, while democracy was nowhere in sight, these schools were in fact rather open, one may even venture to say progressive, in spirit. On the other hand, by the mid-19th century, when the idea of democracy was very much on everyone's mind, these old charter schools, in a wondrous about face, emerged as the most exclusive boarding establishments in the country, with extensive experience in preparing pupils for their future role as the British elite. The name "public" remained however, except that now it was the "fee-paying public," aka the current British elite, who could afford the mammoth sum—the officers and senior administrators of the British Empire, who habitually sent their little offspring on a long voyage back home to be educated as gentlemen. In essence, this education was meant to teach them that it's not whether you win or lose, it's how you play the game. Some learned it better than others.

Tentatively, the unfortunate tykes were also meant to learn classics, as classical training was deemed, again tentatively, the main, in fact almost the only, instrument for training the mind. So rigorous was this training, though, when fastidiously implemented, that only the toughest cerebral constitutions could survive it, with the predictable result that it was very rarely fastidiously implemented, and when it was, was pretty much wasted on the majority of the boys. It must have been then the saying emerged that whenever someone set out to learn what one must and then forgot it all, what was left was culture. An expedient credo in the circumstances when great intellectual zeal was not expected and often looked down upon. To be sure, most upper-class boys were not really sent to public schools to become scholars, but to become reasonably well-educated men of the world, to meet other boys of their class, and to develop "character."

Character development included a charming little custom called "fagging," whereby younger pupils were required to act as personal servants to senior boys. It originated as a result of the 'monitorial system,' a structure for maintaining order in boarding houses, when schoolmasters' authority was practically limited to the classroom only. Senior pupils were given both power over, and responsibility for, the behavior of younger boys, and in a typically feudal fashion, fagging carried with it well-defined rights and duties on both sides. Senior boys, sometimes called fag-masters, were protectors of their fags and responsible for their good conduct. In cases of any problems outside the classroom, such as bullying or other injustice, junior boys' recourse was to them, not to a form-master, and, except in the gravest cases, all incidents were dealt with by fag-masters on their own responsibility.

The tasks undertaken by fags, the time taken, and their general treatment, varied widely from relative freedom to indentured servitude. Each school had its own traditions. Any assortment of duties could be compulsory, such as blacking boots, brushing clothes, cooking breakfasts, running errands, bringing tea to the fag-masters' study, or fagging (assisting) at cricket or football. Also in a typically feudal fashion, fagging may have included *droit du seigneur,* or the right of the first night, and the second, and the third, which is how modern English acquired the present usage of the word. At many schools, fag-masters were expected to reward their fags for their pains by giving a monetary "fag tip." It's not whether you win or lose, it's how you play the game. Husband remained consistently tight-lipped on how he played it.

With time, what with this running of the boys affairs left in the boys' own hands, outdoor activities became more important than academics, and the source of all prestige. While character training steadily overhauled the training of the mind as the prime aim of English education, so games and team sports came to stand for nearly everything that was worth having in the masculine nature. If at some time past intellectual attainments may have been undervalued, they now became highly suspect as presumptive evidence of unmanly character and almost a disgrace in themselves.

By the end of the 19th century, these British boarding schools were as supremely exclusive as they were supremely British. The world was changing though, and other nations were beginning to play a role on the international stage, with the newly rich upstarts from unmentionable countries presuming to give themselves airs and to wish they could give their offspring no worse an education than the British masters of the empire, upon which the sun never set, gave to theirs. Switzerland was becoming their banker; why not their educator as well? No sooner said than done, and Husband's Alma Mater sprung into being with the ease of a well-oiled machine securely built on a tried-out model. It became an international boarding school for boys. Sports came first of course, for which purpose the original campus, which accommodated such indispensable activities as polo and cricket, was soon deemed insufficient, and with time the second one was built, the winter campus, this being Switzerland, whose banks would go insolvent if its bankers and their international clients, along with their children, did not ski.

By the time Husband arrived, in his early teens and in eager search of physical and mental firmness, both campuses were fully operational, churning out future kings, dukes, assorted maharajas and sheiks, as well as sundry gentry and the well-to-do from around the globe.

Oh, East is East, and West is West, and never the twain shall meet,
Till Earth and Sky stand presently at God's great Judgment Seat.
(R. Kipling, *The Ballad of East and West*)

The Earth and Sky of Kipling's mellifluous prediction did stand presently at God's great Judgment Seat at the Swiss establishment, where the twain finally met, and where the prepubescent representatives from East and West quickly adopted the expedient credo of learning and forgetting. With the consequent passage of time, as they grew older, although not necessarily wiser, and indeed forgot most of what they had learned, they did, however, retain an awareness that the world was wide, fascinating, and worth traveling about, which awareness they called culture. Certainly culture enough to muddle through life with.

All the same, Husband's age group, by the time of the travels described in the following pages, was getting a little more forgetful than decorously acceptable, and the school, objecting to this development, insisted on reminding their seasoned graduates, whom they called *les anciens* and meant it, of that time in their lives when the earth was young, the sun perennially shining, and the future full of laughter. It thus encouraged them to reunite, on a regular basis, in various parts of the world. Those who hadn't misplaced (or forgot about) their invitations, came.

The Black Madonna

The first of the following triptych was a visit to a monastery—a bewitching site in the northern Italian community of Biella, in Piedmont, situated among the Alpine splendor, 1200 meters above sea level, and called Santuario di Oropa.

This monastery, according to legend, had its beginning in the 4th century AD, when one Eusebius of Vercelli carried a black wooden statue of the Virgin Mary, carved, according to revelation, as distinct from legend and therefore uncontestable, by Saint Luke, who, apart from carving statues, also dabbled in scribbling, producing the Gospels according to St. Luke. Eusebius, on the other hand, is mostly known for fighting an early Christian heresy called Arianism, which denied the divinity of Christ, seeing that he was born of a mortal woman, as were many Greek heroes (think Achilles, Theseus, Perseus), who were not divine.

It is necessary to emphasize here that the 4th century Arianism (spelled with two i's) had nothing to do with the 20th century Nazism, but rather with its founder, one Arius, a Christian presbyter in Alexandria, Egypt, who, comparing Jesus with his father, Jehovah, saw a number of incongruities.

Apart from being born of a mortal woman, the fact that Jesus was *born* at all was objectionable, for his sire was certainly transcendental and thus ever-present. Nor could Jehovah die, nor feel pain, either physical or emotional. Nor did he sleep, nor eat, nor drink, with the consequent processes of digestion and excretion. That Jehovah did not excrete, Arius was absolutely sure. As sure as he was about Jesus doing all these things in his earthly existence. Arius thus asserted that the Son of God was a subordinate entity to God the Father and found plenty of followers among the polytheistic denizens of the declining Roman Empire, who were traditionally used to gods and mortals copulating, and often wished one such god or goddess descended upon them. All this did not present too much of a problem, though, so long as Christianity was illegal.

The reason it was illegal, in the very tolerant multi-religious society of the Roman Empire, was its own intolerance, for its commitment to monotheism was not self-contained within an ancient and proud race, as was the case with the Hebrews, but fanatically aggressive. Theirs was a proselytizing extremism of a new faith with an unshakable belief in its own righteousness, all in the name of a humble laborer who was crucified as a common criminal, and whose passing left the world apparently unchanged. Him, incomprehensibly, they made into a god and blasphemed against all other gods, and they refused to perform a single patriotic ritual - the sacrifice of a pinch of incense before the statue of a Roman emperor. In addition, their apocalyptic preaching, which maintained that the world was soon to come to an end, made them appear as terrorists against the state, for there was no other world at the time but the Roman world. And yet there was no serious effort to eradicate Christianity until the three-year reign of Decius, one of the short-lived 3rd century Barracks Emperors. Decius was fighting to save an empire that was on the verge of collapse, and he had no tolerance for intolerance. Similar attempts were made by other emperors thereafter, but they were rarely whole-hearted, and never as continuous as the later Church led history to believe. Ultimately, in one of those preposterous inconsistencies with which history abounds, this persecution, instead of weakening the new religion, strengthened it. The willingness of the early Christians to go to their deaths rather than compromise their allegiance to their deity made for a very convincing argument in favor of the uniqueness and power of Christian faith. It weeded out the weak, and it recruited the strong.

By the third century, the desire for martyrdom was almost out of control. Christians deliberately flouted Roman practices—they insulted magistrates and destroyed sculptures of Roman deities in an attempt to provoke arrest and torture, so they may emulate the suffering of Jesus. A competitive spirit developed as to who would die the worse death. They courted martyrdom because martyrs were honored as heroes of faith, and their salvation was assured. It was fervently believed that for one hour of earthly torture the martyr would gain an eternity of immortal bliss. The worse the martyrdom, the wider the gates of Heaven were thrown open to the champion, soon to be elevated into sainthood. Tears of joy welcomed hungry lions in the arena. The anatomical parts the beasts found inedible, became the holiest of relics, treated like precious jewels.

And then, in a cruel twist of fate, it all came to an end. In the early 4th century, emperor Constantine, faced with the inevitability of Christianity's expansion, legalized it, thus ending persecutions. But the early Christians *expected* the world to resist their call for repentance. They taunted it and *hoped* for it to loath their warnings of an imminent apocalypse. When the world suddenly capitulated and embraced their faith, many felt ill used; nay, shaken. Not only the world was no longer prepared to martyr them, which they had come to see as their privilege and their entitlement, but it was offering them license, wealth and power. Things could not have gotten worse. Some, like St. Simeon Stylites, in panic, climbed atop pillars and stayed there for years, in Simeon's case, 37 years. At first, when he wasn't too adept at climbing, he chose a nine-foot pillar, but as his skill increased, so did his pillars, and it is asserted that in the fourth decade of his vertical residence, he looked at the world from fifty feet above the ground. Many centuries later, in 1833 to be exact, Alfred, 1st Baron Tennyson, found the climber saint's activities irresistible and wrote a poem that speaks with Simeon's voice.

> Let this avail, just, dreadful, mighty God,
> This not be all in vain, that thrice ten years,
> Thrice multiplied by superhuman pangs,
> In hungers and in thirsts, fevers and cold,
> In coughs, aches, stitches, ulcerous throes and cramps,
> A sign betwixt the meadow and the cloud,
> Patient on this tall pillar I have borne
> Rain, wind, frost, heat, hail, damp, and sleet, and snow...

Others preferred a horizontal existence, although comparable in torment to Simeon's vertical ordeal, and fled into the wilderness, either Syrian or Egyptian, there to substitute voluntary ascetic activities, of preferably a harrowing nature, for martyrdom. In the scourging desert sun, they hacked their small cells in the raw rock, which took about a year, inside which cells they lived thereafter on dry locust and cold water carried from a nearby oasis. But in wishing to escape worldly temptations, they were sorely disappointed. St. Jerome, the translator of the Scriptures, tried it. In the barren desert parched with fires of the merciless sun he sat, "solitary, full of bitterness; my disfigured limbs shuddered away from the sackcloth, my dirty skin taking on the hue of the Ethiopian's flesh; every day tears; every day sighing, my battered body aching on the naked earth. Yet that same I, the comrade of scorpions and wild beasts, was there, watching the maidens in their dances; my face haggard with  fasting, my mind burnt with desire in my frigid body, and the fires of lust alone leaped before a man prematurely dead." Apparently not quite dead yet, for he soon left for Rome, there to be surrounded, instead of scorpions and wild beasts, by a circle of well-born and well-educated women, including a couple of beautiful young widows from the noblest patrician families. After allegations were brought up against him by the Roman clergy of an improper relationship with one of the widows (as per his vision in the desert), he departed for Antioch, in which ancient city he would spent the rest of his life scribbling, amply provided by said widow with the means of livelihood.

It was for good reason St. Jerome couldn't endure the desert. One of his contemporaries, who also lived an ascetic life in a desert, believed that the Christian hermit's most fearsome enemy was an emotional state he called *accidie*. One of the dangers of solitude, *accidie* was a tedium, or perturbation of the heart, an awesome apathy, boredom, and mental distraction, which debilitated the body and disoriented the mind with delirious visions. And yet the phenomenon endured. Scores flocked to the desert. Often, unable to bear complete solitude, the hermits did their rock hewing in relative proximity to each other, and although still leading separate lives, they at least had the knowledge of similar activity churning nearby, whatever that activity was. The idea that full spirituality was best achieved by renouncing the world, proved highly seductive and came to be known as monasticism.

Meanwhile, in that renounced world far away from the deserts, once the threat of persecution was removed, and church offices became stepping stones to wealth and power, Christians began to fight among themselves. The young faith had yet to resolve many theological questions, and now that it was safe for its adherents to air their differences, cracks widened in the Christian community, with factions accusing one another of heresy, and each claiming to be the sole arbiter of orthodoxy and the leader of the church. Mobs, ever eager for diversion and entertainment, took up the cause of one party against another, and whenever the other cheek was turned, it was hit very hard and blood flowed. Hosanna!—there was once more the chance to validate one's faith through martyrdom.

It was then that the aforementioned Arius, the presbyter in Alexandria, appeared, contesting Christ's divinity with uncontestable arguments. He seems to have been a brilliantly charismatic, if quarrelsome, man, twice excommunicated by the bishop of Alexandria, which damnation deterred him not at all from his eloquent perorations that drew a multitudinous following. The first ecumenical council was soon called to the city of Nicaea, near Constantinople, to which all bishops of the empire were summoned, to resolve the dispute. The bishops, including our Eusebius of Vercelli, dutifully came, saw, but didn't conquer. Resolved to provide a unifying creed that all Christians would profess, which asserted that the Son *was* of the same substance as the Father, and succeeding in ratifying it, they totally failed to convince all Christians to accept it, and the squabbling continued.

It was at about the same time that doubts were heard concerning what was beginning to be seen as still another type of heresy—the excessive and eccentric individualism of the desert hermits—with the impassioned Eusebius willing and ready to fight on both fronts: against Arius of Alexandria, and against the desert deviation. He succeeded at neither. Arianism would not only survive into the 9th century, but will resurface again in the Reformation; and another man, Benedict of Nursia, would become the father of Western monasticism as we know it, which would redirect the eccentrics and make them submit to the Benedictine Order, the first of many monastic orders to follow. The Rule of St. Benedict had the wandering apostates click their heels. Escape the world they still could, but not wander. In the strictly socialized and institutionalized communities of monks, behind thick stone walls, all individualism was ousted and a strict discipline of much prayer, exceedingly hard work, and precious little talk was introduced, leaving the monks little leisure to indulge in tantalizing visions on the model of St. Jerome in his desert.

Yet, leaving Nicaea for Italy at the end of the failed proceedings, and stopping in Jerusalem on the way, Eusebius, our quixotic fighter for the cause, did come across a black wooden statue of the Virgin Mary, and did believe in its having been carved by Saint Luke. With no one objecting to its removal, he took it with him on his voyage west. We shall never know whether he cherished a dream of founding a monastery in Oropa, but we do know (or rather we have been told) that having arrived in Oropa, he placed it into a niche in a big boulder, around which, at a later date, a church was built, and later still, a monastery was founded, where no Arianism was allowed, and to which Husband's alma mater proposed that we become humble pilgrims.

▼

We rented a car in Milan, as per instructions, and drove toward the town of Biella, where we were to meet with the rest of the group, transfer to a coach, and communally go up the mountain by that mode of transportation. This we did, and after the initial greetings, ascent began along an alarmingly narrow and serpentine road that wound round and round, allowing uncomfortably frequent prospects of perpendicular chasms, which distracted from the beauty of the landscape.

The wives were more alarmed by these prospects than the husbands however, for the husbands were too preoccupied in trying to recognize the naughty young companions of their school years behind the wrinkles of unremitting age that testified to unremitting naughtiness. While some of them knew each other from other reunions, others didn't, and those who didn't needed all the assistance they could get.

When finally the monastery rose before our eyes, it took one's breath away. Solemn and pure, an integral part of the mountain slope into which it was set, it seemed carved out of a living rock, majestically overlooking the wooded 1200 meter drop into the valley below. The sky was leaden; one could almost touch the heavy clouds as they hung low above the ground, lending further gravity to the site. There was something primordial about it all. Five thousand years earlier ancient Sumerians firmly believed that the copulation of Earth and Sky produced the primeval Mountain, which forever remained a link between the two. All deities born thereafter lived on mountaintops, where magnificent temples were erected for them by humble worshippers who hoped to moderate their capricious will. We were now gaping at one such temple, and while going unshod was out of the question (much too cold), the ground appeared no less sacred.

All such (or similar) pagan notions were clearly abhorrent to the good old proselytizing Eusebius when he came here to convert the local heathens to the true faith. How ecstatic the heathens were over Eusebius' arrival is uncertain, but it undoubtedly didn't hurt his own reputation in the Christian community to be considered saintly for his zealousness. Self-service has benefited the world as much as vanity and self-indulgence have done. The splendid edifice that eventually arose on the site of his choice was in front of our eyes as a testament to this platitude. And we were certainly the beneficiaries. Not that Eusebius would have given his approbation, for the merry lot that eventually assembled in the courtyard of the monastery must, in spirit, have resembled the original heathens far more than later Christians. One would be hard-put to deny them pleasures of the flesh.

As it was supper time, satisfying the latter began presently. As a special treat, we were led into the Santuario's kitchens, where, in one of the enormous fireplaces, a massive hog was roasting on a gigantic spit, slowly turning round and round by a mechanical device above the blazing fire, and if that sight weren't satisfactory enough, there were heavy medieval tables laden with every offering a self sufficient domain could proffer. There were mountains of fresh eggs in large baskets, a large choice of cheeses—made from cow or goat milk; there were sausages of infinite variety hanging from ancient beams among pots and pans as ancient as the beams, and there were herbs and spices kept in large earthen jars that must have stood on their shelves for the last 500 years.   There were rabbit carcasses on still another table being split apart for a stew whose broth was bubbling on a nearby stove of a herculean size, emitting a wonderful smell, and freshly baked bread of irresistible aroma formed a mount on a table across.   There were fruit and vegetables locally grown, and jugs of wine produced in the monastery vineyards and kept in the monastery's cellars, ready to be taken through into the adjacent refectory by the silent monks in dark habits with huge aprons tied around their frames. There a communal meal was consequently held, fit more for sensual gourmets than for ascetic cenobites.   These monks were not just cooks, they were epicures proud of their skill, which, considering that both pride and love of food were among the Seven Deadly Sins, made me convinced that the dear dead Eusebius was turning in his grave not unlike that hog in the nearby kitchen that was roasting in the fireplace.

But at least Eusebius had the posthumous satisfaction of knowing he was not responsible for this output.   St. Benedict and his Rule were to blame.   Painfully aware of the plight of the desert monks, he proclaimed idleness the enemy of the soul, and further proclaimed prayer and manual labor the two most efficient remedies. *Ora et Labora*—Prayer and Work—became the motto of the Benedictine Rule. The morning bell rung at 3:30 am. Prayer began with Vigils at 4 am and continued throughout the day with Lauds at 6 am, Terce at 9 am, Sext at noon, None at 3, Vespers at 6, Compline at 9. How they knew time before the invention of the clock, or before sunrise, or after sunset, is anyone's guess. I should think it was their guess too, and the hours could not possibly have been correctly observed. But no one was the wiser, and life went on. When the monks did not pray, they worked. Before they died and were buried in the monastery's cemetery, which also served as an orchard on account of its soil's exceptional fertility, they built edifices, lay roads, drained swamps, tilled the land, sowed and reaped, raised livestock, sheared the sheep, weaved, stitched, darned, fished, cooked, washed, etc., etc, from dusk to dawn. And a good thing too, for when the Roman Empire irrevocably fell under the onslaught of the German barbarians from the dark northern forests, and money economy collapsed, these monasteries became self sufficient domains where human life was relatively protected and provided for. Inevitably, whether St. Benedict meant it or not, as with every occupation, which is transmitted from generation to generation, the monks became superb at whatever they did and proud of it, to which our repast, many a century later, testified. Meantime, back in times medieval, more was required of them.

Rome may have fallen, but it was never forgotten, and when three centuries after its fateful collapse, the redoubtable Charlemagne made it easy for himself to unite most of Western Europe for the first time since the Roman Empire by slaughtering half of it, he felt the time had come for the Empire's rebirth. He crossed the Alps into Italy and had himself crowned emperor by Pope Leo III in the old St. Peter's Basilica, thereupon directing his ambitious aspirations to collecting as much information about the old world as he could find. To achieve this purpose, back in Germany, he gathered some of the finest scholars in Europe to his court in Aachen, who expanded monastery schools throughout his domains and promoted the copying of ancient manuscripts whenever and wherever they could find them. This latter activity fell as an additional chore on monks' shoulders. But not before basic literary standards were imposed on them, for with Rome's disintegration, literacy had disintegrated as well, and by Charlemagne's time, few could read and write, including monks and clergy. This development he didn't like at all, feeling "lest perchance, as the skill in writing was less, so also the wisdom for understanding the Holy Scriptures might be much less than it rightly ought to be. And we all know well that, although errors of speech are dangerous, far more dangerous are the errors of understanding." Charlemagne's 'empire' was short-lived, but forever after, in the newly organized monastic scriptoriums, monks collected and copied antique manuscripts, assembling the best libraries of the middle ages, and ultimately preserving ancient knowledge.

Santuario had one such library, rebuilt, augmented and beautified in the Baroque period, when the entire monastery, alas, was rebuilt, augmented and beautified (good thing they left the kitchens alone). It looked like the library from the Beauty and the Beast that Beast gave to Belle as a present. We were allowed a peek after supper, but no more. The librarian had done his 9 pm Compline by then, and was not to be disturbed. The wives were disappointed, the husbands relieved. They had all recognized one another by then; had no difficulty reversing the years; slapped each other's shoulders, "old-man-ning" themselves with a vengeance; and laughed uproariously disturbing the monks in their precarious sleep. En masse, they presently retired to a well-stocked bar that one of them discovered tucked behind an obscure doorway that was open into the wee

145

hours of the morning. The more devoted of the wives accompanied the husbands. Some found it more difficult to get up the following morning than others.

The difficulty was augmented by the blissful freshness of the mountain air, which induced deep and restful sleep, and by the great comfort of monastic beds. Just as St. Benedict, with his vows of poverty, chastity and obedience, which he imposed onto monastic communities, clearly did not mean for the monks to turn into epicures, he also did not mean for them to sleep comfortably, what with the morning bell ringing at 3:30 or thereabouts. (If it rung, we didn't hear it). Yet, on the other hand, he also emphasized hospitality, insisting that "all guests shall be received as though they were Christ." Still, in all my perusals of the Scripture, I never read about Christ sleeping comfortably anywhere; certainly not as comfortably as we did. Our monks' cells, austere and whitewashed they may have been, lacked no amenities. I was left to conclude that we were received *better* than Christ.

We did get up in time though, to a plentiful breakfast washed down with unbelievably delicious unpasteurized milk. There could not have been an hour since it was procured from obliging bovines in the monastery cowsheds, before they were led out to pasture, for the milk was still warm. With one's lips feeling divine liquid flow into one's mouth through the layer of crème fresh, one was in heaven. Breakfast over, and with the taste of nectar and ambrosia lingering in our mouths, we were piled into the same coach that brought us up here, for an excursion to the best-preserved medieval citadel in Piedmont—Ricetto di Candelo. It appeared our organizers felt that before we toured the medieval monastery, from which most medievalism was removed by the overzealous Baroques effort, we needed to be submerged into an unadulterated medieval atmosphere that would help us, the following day, to recreate the original spirit of the religious community. Submerged we were. "Ricetto" is derived from Latin "receptum", which by the late Middle Ages came to mean "shelter." Local peasants built the complex in the 13th century as a safe warehouse for agricultural products. The population retreated inside only in times of danger. A walk over a drawbridge, then through a tower gateway, leads to a small square paved with rounded river stones. The streets slope, enabling water and sewage to run off towards the curtain tower at the end of the central street. The buildings consist of two rooms placed one over the other. The ground floor (caneva) was ordinarily used as a cellar, while upstairs (solarium) served as a warehouse. Because Ricetto has so incredibly survived in its authentic state, walking through it affords an enchanted visitor unique opportunity to feel the atmosphere of the days of yore; silent and peaceful streets convey an incomparable sense of medieval magic, and indeed fortify one with the correct mind-set to tour and feel the spirit of an old monastery that for centuries held sway over the surrounding territory, including Ricetto di Candelo.

No one really knows when the very first structure was built around the statue of the Madonna and Child that St. Eusebius brought all the way from Palestine in the 4th century, or what that structure looked like. It is a pretty big statue, and how the venerable Eusebius managed to transport it all the way across the Mediterranean and up to the top of Monte di Oropa, as the mountain is called, is anyone's guess. But I suppose saintly men are capable of miraculous deeds. For whatever reasons of his own, our Eusebius placed his statue in the middle of the forest, in the niche of a huge boulder, and whoever found her there afterwards and tried to remove her, couldn't do so, as she increased in weight exponentially with time, and became unmovable. She obviously *was* moved eventually, perhaps by another miracle-working saint, since today she resides inside her own Madonna Chapel in the Santuario's Ancient Basilica.

The statue, made of Lebanon cedar, shows the Madonna presenting the Child at the Temple. The faces and hands of both the mother and the child are painted black – hence Black Madonna. If St. Luke, who presumably did have an artistic gift, did carve this Madonna, it needs to be emphasized that in doing so, he committed a very serious religious offence, for the Second Commandment sternly forbid him, along with everyone else, any creation (let alone adoration) of imagery: *"Thou shalt not make unto thee any graven image, or any likeness of any thing that is in heaven above, or that is in the earth beneath, or that is in the water under the earth. Thou shalt not bow down thyself to them, nor serve them..."* Thousands went to their deaths for much less than that, let alone be allowed to write a Gospel and have it accepted as canonical. And Eusebius should have known better than to haul this graven image through half the world in order to have it worshipped. And if this godless act of having been carved and worshipped wasn't enough, someone, for whatever reason, painted her black, although there are no records as to who or why. Of course there are scholarly skeptics who *will* disbelieve, and who date both the sculpture and the paint to the thirteenth century, but as no one wants to spoil a good story with the truth, no one pays them any heed.

It is indeed to the thirteenth century, though, that the earliest surviving parts of the monastery date. A church first replaced whatever building was there originally around the boulder containing the statue, then some adjacent structures appeared, and although most of them were replaced, in the seventeenth century, with the aforementioned unmentionable Baroque edifices, the lower complex is still called the Ancient Basilica. The Madonna having indeed been moved, whether by miracle or force, now resided in the Madonna's Chapel, decorated with delicate frescos illustrating her life, and although the frescos may not be on a par with Giotto's illustrations in Padua, they are certainly lovely.

There one sees the disconsolate Joachim, exiled to the desert for his inability to produce a child, and there is his faithful Anne, back home crying over the same misfortune. Mercifully, they do not cry for long, for—behold!—two rainbow winged angels visit them in their solitude and predict a birth. Presently they reunite at the Golden Gate, where a giddy Joachim plants a kiss on his wife's tear-wet sallow cheek, thus inaugurating the Immaculate Conception, of which Mary was the result. Immaculate Conception does not mean the conception of Jesus, but that of Mary, who was granted unsullied origins in the apocrypha that grew around her lore sometime in the middle ages to keep her worthy of her blameless son. The son's conception is called the Annunciation, and here, on the wall, was seen the naughty archangel sent by his master to kneel before the most virginal of maidens and make her conceive without even a kiss, just words, which for the sake of appearances were given the ornate name of Annunciation. Surely she was to be pitied, for here was the one woman who had to go through all the pain of birth, but to be satisfied with words only, however ornate. The 5th and 6th articles in this little volume describe the process in detail.

As to the Black Madonna herself, as unique as she appeared, she was not in fact unique. There are a number of them, each with her own legend and her own saint logging her from some holy place or other. The Montserrat Abbey in Spain, not unlike our Santuario in either setting or purpose, is one such place. Malta is another, and Naples, and many places in France. All over Europe are there Black Madonnas that seem to have sprung between the twelve and the fifteenth centuries from no one knows where. And because their origin is obscure, the field has been open for all sorts of ingenious explanations.

The most obvious and logical one is that these statues were rescued from burning churches. Because the statues were made mostly of wood, they would darken from heat, and the only way to save face, so to speak, was to paint it black. Of course every rescue was considered "miraculous" and "transformative," and the sculpture's altered aspect would be the visual manifestation of such transformation.

A more highbrow theory has to do with a line from the Song of Songs: " *I am black but lovely, O daughters of Jerusalem, Like the tents of Kedar, Like the curtains of Solomon. Do not stare at me because I am swarthy, For the sun has burned me...*" As the last line proclaims, the word 'black' in Hebrew may not necessarily mean that her skin is racially black, but that she has been burned by the sun. The girl is of rustic birth and has been living in the fields, which is why she is browned with the ruddy health of a country life. This bucolic maiden feels the greatness of the honor to be chosen by a great king (Messiah, in many interpretations), and, surrounded by her friends, daughters of Jerusalem all, with simple modesty sets forth her claim. The parallel between this maiden with her king Solomon and Mary with Jehovah was often drawn, but there is little probability that whoever was carving our Madonnas, knew Hebrew. Latin was the language of the empire, and in Latin the first line reads *Negra sum sed formosa.* Hence the Black Madonna.

Still another explanation maintains a pagan origin. According to this theory, the Black Madonna is the ancient earth-goddess converted to Christianity. Some fertility goddesses were indeed pictured as black from time to time, often carved from black stone, among them Ceres, the Roman goddess of agricultural fertility and her Greek equivalent, Demeter, which derives from *Ge-meter* or Earth Mother. The best fertile soil is black in color and the blacker it is, the more suited for agriculture. In point of fact, there is a tradition in Piedmont, where our Santuario is located, that before the Christians, local Celts had a black fertility goddess whose image they carved and adored. Was she baptized into our Madonna? This possibility is supported by one of the great early Christian figures, Pope Gregory the Great, who, in the year 601 urged the following in a letter to priests: "It is said that the men of this nation are accustomed to sacrificing oxen. It is necessary that this custom be converted into a Christian rite. They shall bring to the churches their animals, and kill them, no longer as offerings to the devil, but for Christian banquets in name and honor of God. Only thus, by preserving for men some of the worldly joys, will you lead them more easily to relish the joys of the spirit." And Gregory the Great, who invented such a user friendly thing as the Purgatory, should know.

But whatever the explanation, there she stands, with her babe on her arm, a mortal maiden with her mortal child, asserting Alexandrian Arius's claim of Christ's mortal beginnings, and defying the good Eusebius who took such pains to combat such notions, and more pains still to bringing her here. In this monastery she stands, whose conception was another man's idea, based on other men's actions, which actions were provoked by other men's deeds, and on and on, in an unending flow of cause and effect, into the deep antiquity she stares, to which she is a silent witness.

The Golden Age

The following year, the school, wishing to upstage the previous year, hired the Al Andalus Express (the Orient Express of Spain) built in France between 1929 and 1930 by the Wagon-Lits Company, and now restored to its original splendor. In it, the Belle Epoque charm mingled with the comfort of the modern age, allowing the traveler the pleasure of the journey that transported one through the wonderful scenery of the southern Iberian Peninsula, the unforgettable Andalusia.

The name Al-Andalus allegedly comes from the Vandals who, having crossed the Rhine in 406 together with other Germanic tribes during their migration, went their own way directly thereafter, and by 409 settled in Roman Spain, calling it Vandalusia. The name was changed to Al-Andalus by the Arabs who arrived in Spain in the early 8th century and stayed for 800 years, leaving there, especially in the south, their indelible mark.

About the time Emperor Justinian, sovereign of the Eastern Roman Empire, called Byzantium, lay dying, a boy was born in a town of Mecca, in Arabia, part of the self same Eastern Roman Empire that stretched, under this Justinian, from southern Spain to Syria and Arabia, and from northern Africa to the Danube, encompassing, if not the entire former Roman world, a good chunk of it. That boy would put an end to that world.

In theory, Mecca had long formed a link between Rome or Constantinople and the East, with the great trade routes ending in the port of Yemen. In practice though, both Romans, and later Byzantines, viewed 'Province Arabia' as a border zone of uncertain status, and traders were more likely to travel the Silk Route through central Asia, which meant that prosperity in the peninsula was far from assured. Consequently, brigandage between nomadic Bedouin tribes was virtually a national institution. In the words of one poet, 'our business is to make raids on the enemy, on our neighbor and on our brother, in case we find none to raid but a brother.' Still, two huge caravans did set out from Mecca to the Yemeni ports twice a year—one in summer, the other in winter—that kept the town going. Another thing that kept it going was its enormous cube-shaped meteorite called Ka'bah that was fervently worshiped by the surrounding tribes. In keeping with their nomadic style, the Bedouins were not especially religious. Their early deities consisted of springs (oases) and rocks. They also worshipped several lunar deities, and there was, in addition, an idol in human form whose idea may have come from Babylon. But the main deity in Mecca, represented by the meteorite, was *allah*, the god. The name Mecca itself came from a word meaning sanctuary, and implied that it was a religious center from the earliest times. Certainly Ptolemy assumed as much when he mentioned it in his *Geography* in mid-2nd century A.D.

Muslims refer to the era before Islam as "the time of ignorance," when there was no attempt to bring together all the disparate myths and legends scattered across Arabia. Yet it was, perhaps, this very divergent nature of their early beliefs that helped give Islam, when it did appear, such an immediate appeal. Another contributing factor was a ring of monotheism encircling Arabia. There had long been a community of Jews in Yemen, and Abyssinia had by now been converted to Christianity, with the narrow Red Sea criss-crossed on a regular basis by the inhabitants of both shores.

Very little is known about Muhammad except that he was born toward the end of the 6th century. The first biography is supposed to have been written a hundred years after his birth and well after his death, but it is known only through a much later edition of 833, that claims the first one existed. Whether it did or not, much lore had developed since then, including the fact that Muhammad's relatives were the custodians of certain relics related to the Ka'bah, and that the family may have had some pre-Islamic religious prestige. His father died when he was very young, and at twelve he was taken by his uncle to Syria, where he is supposed to have met a Christian monk who influenced him deeply. At twenty five he married his employer, "a wealthy and high-minded widow, fifteen years his senior." He continued to help run her business in the caravan trade for a time, but it was the leisure afforded by this marriage that allowed Muhammad to spend time in a small cave outside Mecca, called Hira.

Records remain silent as to why he felt compelled to leave a comfortable bed with the comfortable high-minded widow upon it and wander outside the city walls to a bare inhospitable cave. Clearly, in a congested world of a small Arab town, where privacy was hard to come by, he needed to do something hush-hush that others may have disapproved, but records remain equally silent as to what exactly it was. These cave visits seem to have gone on for years, when one day he heard a voice telling him to holt whatever he was doing and to keep his hands busy with writing instead. He obeyed, and began to record all the instruction he received, by scratching it on whatever debris lay nearby.

Later these scratchings were collected into a book, the Qur'an. It took a while, however, to gather all the palm leaves, stones, bones and bits of parchment, on which the scattered versions of the 'book' were presumably scratched. Three hundred years will elapse after Muhammad's death before the authorized version of the Qur'an would be finalized by a couple of viziers, who had long lost sight of any scratchings and relied on other sources instead, whatever those were. Despite this, the faithful Muslim fervently believes that every letter in the Qur'an was dictated to Muhammad by the archangel Gabriel (Jibril they call him), and is therefore the inspired word of God. The fact that it is written in Arabic is also important, for the same faithful Muslim, unaware that Arabic was a relatively late derivation from Aramaic, is convinced that it is the language of God and is the tongue spoken in Paradise. Adam and Eve originally spoke Arabic too, but forgot it and were punished by being made to learn the inferior Hebrew.

At Muhammad's death in 633, Islam was confined to the Arabian peninsula. Within barely a hundred years, in an unprecedented expansion, it had grown to the point where its borders touched India in the east, the Atlantic ocean in the west, the heart of Africa in the south, and Byzantium in the north. Its attraction lay partly in the certainties it offered; in the fact that, in its early years it was a tolerant religion; and partly for entirely practical reasons—it taxed people a lot less than the Byzantines did. Also, in its ideals it was a far simpler faith than, say, Christianity. It was egalitarian, and there was in theory no clergy, no Church, and no rank in which some were more privileged, or closer to God, than others. To begin with, the leadership was not even hereditary. After the Prophet's death, when a new leader was needed, the institution of the caliphate immerged, *Khalifa* meaning a successor and a deputy. The first three caliphs were related neither to each other, nor to Mohammad. Despite this, and despite the fact that two out of three were assassinated, their period in office would always be venerated. However, the fourth caliph, Ali, was Muhammad's son-in-law and cousin and, in offering himself for election as caliph, he was reverting to a pre-Islamic tradition of heredity. Ali's followers became known as *Ali, shi'atu, Ali* that in time was collapsed into *Shi'a*, which would become very influential, but not quite yet, for Ali, too, was assassinated. In the Islamic civil war that ensued, the victor was a leader of the Meccan clan of Umayya, whose followers would later be called *Sunni*. The immediate difference between the Shi'a and the Sunni was that the Shi'a believed the caliphate should consist of the blood descendants of Mohammad, while

159

the more egalitarian Sunni did not. Other differences would emerge in time, over which untold blood will be spilt.

The Umayyad victory was no surprise, as they were very astute political, administrative and intellectual leaders. In Damascus they set up their capital, from which they would expand the Arab territories from the shores of the Atlantic to the Hindus river, replace Roman and Byzantine coins with Arabic ones, build the Dome on the Rock in Jerusalem, and create the first Arabic centers of learning where the first grammars and dictionaries were compiled as the Arabic language came under systematic study. This marked Islam's emergence as a major civilization in its own right, whose extraordinary intellectual thirst was matched only by its astonishing geopolitical expansion.

Meantime the dissenting religious, political, and social groups of the Shi'a were gathering strength, and toward mid-8th century, under the leadership of the 'Abbāsids, descendants of the Prophet's uncle Al-'Abbās, they rose against the Umayyads' easy-going and by now unapologetically self-serving rule. After years of inconclusive civil war in Syria and Iraq, a great banquet was arranged by the 'Abbāsids, ostensibly to mend their differences with the Umayyads, attended by all the most important members of both clans. To this banquet the 'Abbāsids, in an unconscionable show of bad manners, brought hidden weapons, having by then decided upon the most efficient way to mend differences by massacring all the Umayyads in attendance. Abu'l-'Abbās, the leader of the Shi'a sect was voted caliph by his troops, and the new dynasty came into force. This watershed development was marked by moving the capital. Damascus was replaced with a brand-new city, situated on the western bank of the Tigris river in what is now Iraq, near a small town that had been there for centuries, by the name of Baghdad. The 'Abbāsid caliphate of Baghdad would endure for half a millennium.

The name Baghdad means "Given by God," but it was also known as "Round City" because of its circular form. Allegedly, it was built in four years by a hundred thousand laborers, craftsmen and architects. By 800, although less than half a century old, Baghdad had grown from nothingness to a world center of international significance, standing alone as a rival to Byzantium. The royal palace occupied the third of the city, and the luxury contained within was legendary. Processions sent out to meet foreign dignitaries would boast a hundred lions, and in the Hall of the Tree, mechanical silver birds chirped automatically from gold and silver branches.

The harbors of the city were occupied by ships from China, Africa and the Indies. From all over the world, people flocked to Baghdad. Inside the city, a great variety of languages, in addition to Arabic, was spoken: Greek, Syriac, Aramaic, Sanskrit, and others. Its position was within easy reach of Syria, and, most importantly, Greece and the former Hellenistic world, where learning never died, as it had died in the West. Soon an intensive program of translation into Arabic from Greek and Indian medical, geometrical, and other scientific manuscripts was begun. To give them credit, the 'Abbāsids continued where the Umayyads left off (were forced, by slaughter, to leave off).

The two greatest 'Abbāsid caliphs were Harun al-Rashid and his son al-Ma'mun, in the late 8th and early 9th centuries. Harun al-Rashid was a contemporary of

Charlemagne, the Frankish king of the previous article, who urged his ignorant clergy to acquire literacy, and had scriptoria set up in numerous monasteries. To him, as a special present, Harun al-Rashid sent an elephant, Abul Abbas by name, who, in the spring of 801, lumbered into the streets of Aachen, an old Roman town in western Germany that Charlemagne had chosen as his capital a few years earlier. One can only imagine the thrill that

met the arrival of the enormous creature. History is silent as to how the caliph managed to get him there. Did he walk from Baghdad to Aachen with his trainer on his back?! Europe did not see elephants since Hannibal invaded Italy in the 3rd century B.C., and Germany *never* saw them. By the time he died in 810, Abul Abbas had become a household name in both France and Germany.

But Harun al-Rashid's true renown lies in being the first caliph of the Arab Golden Age. He established libraries and centers of learning, based largely on Greek models discovered during the Arab conquests of Alexandria and Antioch, and while Europe, for the most part, was wallowing in muck, deep ignorance and subhuman survival, Harun al-Rashid's physicians, astronomers, mathematicians and philosophers conducted chemical experiments, astronomical observations, mathematical analyses, and of course teaching. They took it for granted that the earth was round.

Harun al-Rashid is also the protagonist of the most famous of all Arabic literary works, *A Thousand and One Nights*. Unlike science and mathematics, the Arabs did not interested themselves overmuch in Greek literature. They felt their own literary tradition was good enough. Even before they were united by Islam, along with archery and horsemanship, eloquence completed the three basic attributes of a 'perfect man' in the Bedouin Arabia. Although nomads without a settled civilization, they early distinguished themselves in poetry. "The beauty of a man," says one of their endless proverbs, "lies in the eloquence of his tongue," and the rhythm and rhyme, the very music of words, gave the Arabs goose bumps, producing in them what they called "lawful magic" (*sihr halal*). Indeed, they invented the rhyme, which is said to have echoed the swaying of a camel as it moved through the desert, and so enchanted were they with their new invention, that they would later compose legal treatises in rhyme.

Of Harun al-Rashid's son, Al-Ma'mun, it is said that he had a dream—possibly the most fortunate and important dream in history—in which Aristotle appeared. As a result of this dream Al-Ma'mun sent envoys as far afield as Constantinople, in search of as many Greek manuscripts as they could find, and to establish in Baghdad the House of Wisdom, the greatest of all learning and research centers, an Arab Library of Alexandria. There, Aristotle's *Physics* was translated, as well as Plato's *Republic*, along with books on anatomy by Gallen, and works of Hippocrates, Dioscorides,

Euclid, Archimedes, Ptolemy, Apollonius and a host of other Greek scholars.

Al-Ma'mun had an open mind. Not everyone agreed that the Qur'an was solely the work of God. In the middle of the 8th century, there emerged a semi-secret school of thinkers, the Mu'tazilites, who were rationalists obsessed with reconciling the text of the Qur'an and the criteria of human reason. (Five centuries will elapse before Thomas Aquinas, in Paris, will attempt the same with the Bible). Mu'tazilites called almost all aspects of Islam into question. For example, if God is transcendental, He has no human attributes, and the Qur'an could not therefore have been spoken by Him. It must have been created in some other way. Also, if God is just, men must have free will—otherwise, to judge men for acts they are not responsible for, would be unjust. On the whole, the Mu'tazilites held that doubt was the first requirement of knowledge, and their way of thinking appealed to Al-Ma'mun, who promoted their view into a state attitude. Openness and toleration thus run high through Baghdad's golden age. Merchants, theater types, writers, poets and scientists flocked to the city, as they would flock to Berlin, Paris, New York and London in later centuries.

Insha'Allah!—nothing lasts forever, and the great openness did not last forever. By mid-11th century, the fields of study derived from Greek and Indian origin were being called "foreign sciences" by the pious, and slowly but surely, the reassertion of faith against the inroads of science and philosophy turned the society inward. Soon thereafter, the Seljuk Turks, who had come from the region of the Jaxartes River (known today as *Syr Darya*), and having converted to Islam in mid-10th century, took Baghdad. The Seljuks allowed the 'Abbāsid caliphs to serve as religious figure heads, but their sultans (shultana—governor) assumed the responsibility for running Baghdad's empire and defending Islam against its primary enemy, the Christian crusaders. It won't be long, though, till the Mongols hordes will invade in the 13th century, burn, rape, pillage, and slaughter the last caliph. In time, they too will convert to Islam and establish their own civilization, but it will *never* compare to the one they defaced.

Meantime, a very similar civilization, despite Christian inroads, was still flourishing more than 2,000 miles away in Spain.

Back at that ill-fated (for the Umayyads) banquet, one of the Umayyads, 'Abd al-Rahmān ibn Mu'āwiiya by name (eventually called al-Dākhil, the Incomer), escaped the assassins, and in 755 reached Al-Andalus where he found support with the Arabs whose fathers and grandfathers crossed the Straits of Gibraltar back in 711, overrunning most of Visigoth Spain in less than three years. Here al-Dākhil established the Umayyad dynasty that, with its capital in Cordoba, and its own learning centers, research facilities, hospitals, and literary and philosophical feats, was destined to become the envy of the world on par with Baghdad. When, in the tenth century, its ruler assumed the title of caliph, signifying succession to the rule of the Prophet Muhammad, it challenged the pretences of Baghdad itself. When, in the second Christian millennium, Europe began, slowly, very slowly, to wake up from its deep sleep of uncouthness and ignorance, it was to Spain it looked for enlightenment. It was in Spain the works of Aristotle and other Greek philosophers could be found, long since translated into Arabic. It was through the remnants of that world that our train would now take us.

▼

No inquiries were required at the Seville Terminal. The century-old, beautifully restored *La Belle Epoque* train stood out among sleek post-modern high-speed trains that foamed at the mouth like race horses at the gate. The Andalusian, however, would clearly rather stay put and not be bothered. Rushing about was a bore. Bad enough to be born in the 20th century (it could pick a better one out of a top hat); to be jump-started into the 21st was unconscionable. The train was to demonstrate its convictions in the days to follow.

My research, prior to the trip, was nothing short of thorough. I watched *Murder on the Orient Express* at least half a dozen times. God bless my foresight. The Lauren Bacalls were everywhere, and the Jacqueline Bissets, beautifully murderous (murderously beautiful?) one and all. And, of course, the Michael Yorks and Sean Connerys at various stages of life. The well-seasoned variety is a personal preference. Conspicuous absence of an Hercule Poirot was a disappointment. The organizers clearly had not included manslaughter in the program, thus rendering Finney's presence unnecessary. With the exception of this one oversight, however, every detail was attended to.

The lot of us differed from the high-speed passengers as much as our train differed from theirs. No rushing, thank you kindly, Champagne was to be had first—on the platform, before boarding. Ours was the only train that was late in departing. It was a little tipsy.

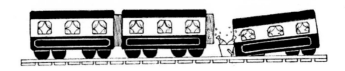

In the golden Andalusian triangle of Cordoba —Granada—Seville, Cordoba was the first stop.

In order truly to understand Cordoba of the 10th century, the period of its greatest cultural and political summit, one must imagine a beautiful, beguiling city with half-a-million population - the biggest, most advanced and civilized city the West had ever seen, fuelled by a prosperous and diverse economy, where highly skilled artisans in leather, textiles, glazed tiles, and an infinite variety of other crafts, all found plenty of employment. One must further visualize a city full of dazzling mosques, libraries, observatories and aqueducts. There was also a university, with a hospital attached, inhabited by deeply learned scientists, erudite writers, poets, artists and wise philosophers. Cordoba produced two of the most celebrated of all Al-Andalus scholars, the Muslim Averroës, and the Jewish Maimonides, who, like their predecessors, the Mu'tazilites of Baghdad, are best remembered for their efforts to harmonize religious faith with reason using Aristotelian philosophy. It had an opulent, dazzling, open-minded princely court in whose brilliant tourneys the whole city participated, and which welcomed scholars independently of their cultural or religious affiliations. Jews, continuously persecuted in Christian lands, found warm reception in Cordoba, where they built a stunning synagogue with a Jewish quarter surrounding it.

Much of the medieval city has disappeared, but much still stands, most notably the astonishing Great Mosque of Cordoba, an architectural wonder and the only place in the world where one can worship Mass in a mosque should one be so inclined. It is surrounded by an intricate web of winding streets lined up with white-washed stucco houses from whose walls cascades of multicolored geraniums spill onto the cobbled stones and into cool intimate patios.

Enchanted, we stood in the middle of this mosque. One could only wonder about the genius who conceived this Islamic hall of mirrors, where a potentially monotonous labyrinth of superimposed horseshoe arches explodes into a wild multi-dimensional maze; where the constant echo of arches and the seemingly unruly staccato of colors both confuse and excite, giving the interior an almost carnavalesque  quality. What sort of a subconscious collective experience could produce art of such astonishing complexity, subtlety and humor?

Ibn Hawqāl, a tenth century geographer from Baghdad, visited Cordoba, and snob though he was about any place other than his native city, he was deeply impressed with Cordoba's intellectual ferment, artistic production, its manufacture and its international trade. Before Cairo was founded, only Constantinople and Baghdad challenged Spain in the variety of exotic products. Al-Andalus was now perceived by the rest of the world as a rich and remote frontier where license, wealth, and unprecedented refinement abounded. Significantly, works of art and architecture, as signs of wealth and cultivation, were at the center of such myths.

Here's one story by Ibn Hawqāl that comes from an extraordinary book compiled by one al-Zubayr in the latter part of the eleventh century. It tells of an exceptional object alleged to have been discovered in Saragossa by a treasure hunter (antique dealer in today's terms). This was a small bronze jar, within which was hidden a small glass jar. A black ring with a carving of a sexually aroused monkey was hidden inside the glass jar. A man who put the ring on his

 finger would have an erection. (A medieval Viagra; I wonder if our draconian Food and Drug Administration would approve it today.) When the ring was taken off, the erection subsided. (Maybe the FDA would approve it.) The Arab nobleman from Sicily who bought the jar from our antiquarian friend carried out one of the meanest practical jokes of all times by giving it to one of his eunuchs. Alfred Hitchcock, who loved nasty practical jokes, would have loved this one. The eunuch didn't. Deeply disheartened, he broke the ring, and it became ineffective. What a waste.

From Cordoba, the train unhurriedly moved toward Granada, using every excuse to stop and relax. The train was lazier than we were. Certainly took longer siestas, during which it snored. Cross my heart. We never had to worry

about the proverbial 'being late for the train'; this one took its sobriquet "civilized" very close to heart. It slept whenever it could, except on those evenings when we dined elsewhere and returned late, when it made sure to wait up and express its scorn at not being taken along.

En route, meanwhile, the fates placed together at dinner two modern Ibn Hawqāls, whose passion for geography and whose snobbism about knowing it better than anyone else certainly equaled those of the good old Persian. The two were my very own husband and another ancien (an alumnus), from a different graduating year, whom Husband didn't know. The introductions behind us, and half way through soup, our chance dinner companion cheerfully asked Husband to name the capital of a certain American state. Husband coughed in his soup, but quickly and mercifully realized there was no reason his interlocutor should know we reside in that state, and cordially gave the answer. Saskatchewan was shot at him next. Husband loosened his necktie and threw Belize back. Eureka!—the reply was Belize City, which was formerly correct, but no longer. Belmopan was now the capital of Belize. Neighboring tables were beginning to turn around with wagering on their minds. I heard Swaziland thrown at Husband; his mouth opened, but nothing came out. He was unequal to Swaziland. "Mbabane!" was roared at him. Husband's eyes were becoming bloodshot: Kyrghizia! Ha! No answer. Bhutan was swung back at him. Not only did this continue through dinner and dessert, but all throughout the trip, whenever those two came into contact, peculiar sounds came out—Lilongwe, Thimphu, Paramaribo. I was paramariboed out.

The centralized system of government developed by the Umayyad princes did not last. In a sense, they had been too successful—the land they had conquered was too vast and rugged to control and govern. By the beginning of the eleventh century at least fourteen different districts declared independence. Under the rule of the so-called party-kings, the hitherto minor provincial areas, the *Taifa* kingdoms, became centers of literature and culture, each boasting a distinct character and tradition.

"After the breaking of the necklace and the scattering of its pearls, the kings of small states divided among themselves the patrimony of the Umayyads." (Ash-Shankandi)

None profited more from Cordoba's downfall than Granada, which recreated the older city's splendor while even surpassing it in refinement. Granada's history reads like a thriller. After the fall of Cordoba, Muslims sought refuge in Granada, where Mohammed ibn Yusuf ibn Nasar had set up an independent emirate, destined to become the final remnant of Islamic Al-Andalus, ruled from the increasingly lavish Alhambra palace for 250 years.

Among many tales that are told of this magical palace, one attracts particular attention, especially when an enchanted visitor beholds the dark rust spots (purported to be blood stains) on the fountain in the middle of the Hall of the Abencerrages.

In the 15th century, a violent rivalry developed over Granada succession. It was actually a harem war between two wives, but it was fought by men. One of the two warring faction supported the ruling emir, Abu al-Hasan who, at an advanced age took a new wife, the young and beautiful

Christian captive, Isabella de Solis, better known by her Muslim name Zoraya. She birthed him two sons and wished for one of them to succeed his father. The other faction supported Boabdil, the son from the emir's earlier union with his cousin, the Princess Ayxa la Horra. Ayxa was the daughter of the previous ruler of Granada (the emir's uncle), Sultan Muhammad Nazar. During his own reign, Muhammad Nazar elevated one loyal family, that of the Abencerrages, to the highest positions, thus earning an even greater devotion on their part. Whatever his misfortunes (five times he lost and regained his throne), the Abencerrages always remained loyal.

Washington Irving, in his *Tales of the Alhambra*, talks of this most ancient and noble line that had its origins with the Umayyads of Syria, and came to Granada after the disintegration of the Cordoba Caliphate. When they witnessed the emir spurn Ayxa and her son in preference of the foreigner Zoraya, the Abencerrages rallied to the support of Muhammad Nazar's daughter and grandson. History repeats itself. Invited to a banquet at the palace for ostensible reconciliation, the leaders of the Abencerrages were slain by the treacherous emir. The place where it happened is called today the Hall of the Abencerrages. The blood stains are still there upon the fountain.

An incongruous tale to be thinking about while observing one of the anciens, standing next to the fountain, wholly oblivious of the stains, and clearly making a killing of his own with a cellular pressed securely to his ear.

Not all the Abencerrages leaders attended the fateful banquet, though, and those who lived continued intrepid, with the result that in the end, Ayxa's son Boabdil did succeed to the throne, only to lose it, in the apocalyptic year 1492, to the most Christian monarchs, Ferdinand and Isabella, who ended forever the golden age of Spanish Islam. Those Jews and Muslims who refused to convert were expelled, and in an interesting development, Zoraya's sons, in the last struggle for Granada, submitted to the conquerors, abandoned their faith and accepted Christianity. They and their offspring intermarried with the Spanish families, were rewarded with land and honors, and imprinted their names upon the Spanish nobility. The Abencerrages, in the words of Mr. Irving, "remained true to their faith, true to their king, true to their desperate cause, and went down with the foundering wreck of Muslim domination, leaving nothing behind them but a gallant and romantic name in history."

A visit to Andalusia cannot be accomplished without a stopover at a vineyard, and on the way back to Seville, where our "golden age" triangle would be finalized, the region of Jerez de la Frontera was duly visited, which is the birthplace of the famous Sherry wines, also spelled Xérès or Jerez. To give it a brief history, wine had been produced here for over three millennia, and around the year "Zero" it began to be exported to Rome for Augustus's table. In the twelfth century, these southern Spanish wines were particularly popular in England, where Eleanor of Aquitaine must have drugged her Henry with them to get her way. He finally decided against similar manipulation, however agreeable, and locked her up for sixteen years. Older than her husband by eleven years to begin with, she still managed to outlive him by another fifteen, living till 82. It's all those delicious medicinal wines that Eleanor must have continued to imbibe, while Henry stopped, that endowed her with such extraordinary longevity in the age when the average life span rarely extended past 40. Should anyone be interested in the particulars of this relationship, and is too bored with endless historical records, James Goldman's play *The Lion in Winter* with the incomparable Katharine Hepburn and the unrivaled Peter O'Toole as the bickering royal couple, is most highly recommended. The bickering is unsurpassed.

The present name "Sherry" came from the original Moorish name of the city, "Sherish." The bodegas (wine

cellars) of Jerez have a great tradition and are irresistible tourist attractions. We went to the González Byass winery, previously visited by the likes of Erté, an expatriate from St. Petersburg, Russia, known to the initiated as Romàn Petròvich Tỳrtov, a sublime designer from a century ago, who did a quick drawing on a wine barrel, of the González Byass's famous Tío Pepe design of a sombreroed gentleman with a guitar. It has been reverently preserved by the proprietors.

In addition to its ancient tradition, the fabulous quality of it wine, and the Erté drawing, the vinery has something else they are proud of. It is a couple of mice that come every night for their cheese and sherry, which are laid out for them of an evening by the aforementioned proprietors. These are the King and Queen of mice, proud of their pre-eminence, even if slightly inebriated after their late evening repast, who bequeath their privilege, at the end of their comfortable lives, to the next lucky generation.

The train whistled a hoot of relief when it slowly pulled into its cozy, familiar spot in the Seville terminal. Halleluiah! No more moving for a while.

Christopher Columbus's remains are preserved in Seville's great cathedral, where they are deposited for eternity in an impressive sarcophagus, with great knightly allegories of the kingdoms of Castille, Aragon, Navara and Leon as pole bearers. Curiously, his remains are also preserved in the Dominican Republic, where a towering lighthouse, built for the purpose in Santo Domingo, keeps the discoverer of the New World securely stored. Perhaps because Columbus was as great a voyager in death as he was in life, his bones may have gotten mixed up along the way. First, his corpse was buried in Valladolid, Spain, where he died. Three years later he was moved to a convent in Seville. But because during his life he had expressed a desire to be buried in the New World, in another thirty years he travelled to Santo Domingo, Hispaniola (Dominican Republic) to be interred there. When, at the end of the 18th century, Spain seceded Hispaniola to France, it kept Columbus by sending him to Spanish Havana. Fast-forward another century, and from Havana, which was by now in the objectionable American hands, he went back to Seville, to repose in the lofty sarcophagus. At about the same time as his bones went back to Spain, however, an inconvenient box was found in Santo Domingo with inconvenient words, "The illustrious and excellent man, Don Colon, Admiral of the Ocean," inscribed on the lid. Whence the box came, no one knows. Whether a few bones (toes? fingers? ribs?) stayed in Santo Domingo while the rest went on, no one knows. In which of the two places the real man (or what's left of him) really is, no one knows. But the arrangement is very convenient for picture-taking, for whether one finds himself in the New World, or the Old, there is an opportunity for such memory-creating in either, as it should be, considering the man belonged to both.

There is still another champion venerated in Seville, although no sarcophagus is on view for the purpose. But he is in everyone's heart, for every Sevillian knows that his/her city was founded by Hercules. Yet not every Sevillian knows that his/her hero did it while obtaining the Golden Apples of the Hesperides, the eleventh out of the twelve labors he had to perform for the nasty king Eurystheus. He was originally supposed to perform ten labors, but the objectionable Eurystheus didn't count the Hydra and the Augean stables, considering them improperly done, and sent Hercules to the Hesperides, and then to the underworld to face Cerberus, to make up for the other two. History, or rather it's fraternal twin, mythology, remains silent as to why Hercules did not object, opening the field for whoever wishes to make up a plausible explanation.

The Hesperides Gardens were located in the far western part of the world, and its golden apples belonged to Zeus as a wedding gift Hera had given him when they tied the knot, so surely the task was impossible, for how can anyone defray a god (*the* god) of his property. Yet Hercules did it, although not without the help of Atlas who lived across Gibraltar in the Atlas Mountains. So unforgettable were the Hesperides, that once Hercules became god in his own right, he planted his own gardens nearby, this time with golden oranges that would with time become known as Seville oranges. Having tasted human food while he was half human, he didn't much care for nectar and ambrosia, and preferred the tangy, delicious marmalade made from Seville oranges.

He also loved the city he founded, which saw the full play of human folly in the passage of numerous civilizations as he watched it from above, and which took the best from each culture. It is indeed a veritable garden, where orange trees exude extraordinary fragrance, and climbing honeysuckle, hydrangea, forsythia, lilac and clematis burst out in fireworks of magnificent color as they hug whitewashed walls of the magical Moorish courtyards, emanating redolent aroma that, mixing with the scent of orange trees, turns the city into a fairy land right out of Harun al-Rashid's *A Thousand and One Nights*.

Oh peoples of Al Andalus!
What Joy is yours!
You have water, shade, rivers and trees;
Paradise itself resides in your dwellings,
And had I to choose,
Here I should remain.
(Ibn Jafays)

177

Ancient Mariners

'The ship was cheered, the harbour cleared,
Merrily did we drop
Below the kirk, below the hill,
Below the lighthouse top.

The Sun came up upon the left,
Out of the sea came he!
And he shone bright, and on the right
Went down into the sea.

(Rhyme of the Ancient Mariner, Samuel Taylor Coleridge)

We timed it. Every 15 minutes Stromboli ejaculated fireworks of molten lava into the star-studded blackness of the night. In the intervals it lazily dripped red onto the dark rocky slopes, only to be guessed at from the upper deck of the five-masted clipper that was circling the primordial isle, struck silent by the sheer majesty of the spectacle. The tranquility of a timeless night lay on the place like a hoary benediction.

There were a lot of us this time, about two hundred, who had sailed from the Roman port of Civitavecchia three days earlier, aged pre- to post mature, what with all the children and parents of the anciens present. This being summer, the alumni were particularly thrilled to bring children, who could not accompany their parents to their various destinations during school terms.

The first day was spent trying to find our bearings on this beautiful vessel that was to sail around the Boot, then up the Croatian cost and on to Venice, carrying us, the ancient mariners that we were, on a pilgrimage to the Never Never Land.

Safely encased in our modern age with all its civilized amenities, hygiene not the least of them, I have always idealized the Middle Ages and its pilgrimages. It is very convenient to be idealistic about the past (or the future). I cannot recommend it enough. One has the conceit of daring without the inconvenience of danger, which provides one with an inestimable amount of self-worth. With this in mind, if I did live back in the Middle Ages, and were granted by God robust enough health to endure its grime, filth, and vermin, I would have spent most of my time on the way to Rome, as I try to do living in the 21st century. The pilgrims leave all their cares at home, the anxieties of their assets or their debts and take only their sins with them (which were in plentiful supply on this boat). Most of these men and women, knowing deep in their hearts that piety begins where passion ends, and that principles are strongest where temptations are most rare, could scarcely be charged with either excessive piety or unwarranted principles. The valiant Odysseus, Aeneas, and Jason, who all sailed and sinned upon these waters millennia before, would have been proud of us. No temptation was to be resisted.

▼

What with Homer's nebulous geography, it is quite possible that the isle of Ponza, our first port of call, was home to the stunning, intelligent and, by extension, treacherous nymph Circe, who lured men with promises of various delicacies which, when eaten or drunk, turned the poor innocents into appalling quadrupeds. With the exquisite sense of meanness the nymph left them their human intelligence, that they may know exactly what had happened to them, allowing her to rejoice at the spectacle of their suffering. So it happened with the reconnoitering party that Odysseus sent ahead on arriving at the island, which was presently turned into swine—except one, who, not having entered Circe's house to taste her offerings, saw what happened to his companions and in horror fled back to the ship. The news so appalled Odysseus, that having thrown caution to the wind, he at once started for the nymph's abode. He wasn't acclaimed Hero for nothing—how remarkable to have this confidence—surely he must have known deep down that he *was* Odysseys, and that the great Olympian gods were not about to allow him to be turned into a pig. To be lost at sea—yes; to be wounded—of course; not to see his wife and son for two decades—certainly; but to be turned into a swine—NO. Sure enough, Hermes, the messenger of the gods, met him on the way, disguised as a young man, of that age when youth looks its loveliest. Presently Odysseus decided the swine weren't going anywhere, while he may never see this attractive young man again. At the end of the rewarding encounter the attractive young man, along with his gratitude, gave our hero a herb—an antidote to Circe's offerings. He also instructed him that when he drank the cup Circe presented him, he must threaten to run her through with his sword unless she freed his friends. No threats were necessary in the end. When Circe used on Odysseus the magic which had always hitherto worked, and to her amazement saw him stand unchanged before her, she so marveled at the man who could resist her enchantment that she loved him and was ready to do whatever he asked of her. Lucky man—beloved by all. She did change Odysseus's companions back into humans of course, but Circe had other victims, the ones who came to the island before Odysseus. For those others Odysseus couldn't care less, as he was not a lover of humanity—only of his companions—and they remained unaltered, destined to live out the rest of their days as beasts. There were also many others who came after Odysseus and encountered a similar fate.

By the time we arrived a couple of millennia later, however, Circe had clearly found herself a different speck of land in the wine-dark sea, for she wasn't there,  and we were safe. The nymph's legacy lived on, though, for her victims, in a counter-evolutionary process, continued to devolve over the interminable centuries, until they returned to the sea in the form of jellyfish. And nasty little amoebas they were, as a number of us had a chance to discover while bathing, swimming, or scuba diving in the gentle coastal waters. One may even suspect human intelligence behind their jellied appearance, considering the vengeance with which they were taking out on us their millenarian frustration.

▼

Capri made one forget all injury. It's not called the Isle of Dreams for nothing. The rugged landscape, luxuriant vegetation, the rocky islets eroded into fantastical shapes by the waves, transform reality into magic. It is one of those places where history and mythology blend. One loses the sense of chronology and bemusedly feels as much a modern sightseer as a visitor of yore. Vergil talks of an ancient race of Teleboans, of Greek origin, living on the island at the time when his hero Aeneas, having perfidiously abandoned the disconsolate queen Dido back in Carthage, came to Italy to sire the new race that was destined to rule the world.

Nor Oebalus, shalt thou be left unsung,
From nymph Semkethis and old Telon sprung,
Who then in Teleboan Capri reign'd;
But that short isle th' ambitious youth disdain'd
And o'er Campania streth'd his ample sway...
(Vergil's *Aeneid,* Book VII. Trans. John Dryden)

This old Telon, at some untold date, thinking "less is more," left the mainland and migrated with his Teleboans to

Capri. The Teleboans were pirates, and the island's situation in the middle of the sea gave them perfect protection from other pirates, as well as a brilliant strategic headquarters from which to raid those other pirates before those other pirates raided them. Telon's son Oebalus, however, dissatisfied with the smallness of his domain, and preferring "more is more" to his father's "less is more," moved back to Campania, with unfortunate results for himself and his people, for Aeneas made quick work of them on his way to Latium.

This Aeneas was the son of the goddess Venus and the prince Anchises, second cousin to King Priam of Troy, also of divine derivation. Venus, loving her son as only a mother could, despite his obvious shortcomings, saved him first from Diomedes of Argos, who nearly killed him, then from Achilles, who badly wounded *her*, and finally helped him flee from smoldering Troy. He escaped with his father Anchises on his shoulders and his son Julius's hand firmly held in his own. Or perhaps it was Ascanius's hand that was firmly held in his own. Or Euryleon's. Aeneas's son appears to have had several names, out of which the Romans, and particularly one Roman family, ultimately preferred "Julius" for reasons explained anon. His wife Creusa Aeneas abandoned to the fire, as he would later abandon Dido to her own fate in Carthage. Aeneas was a man with a purpose, and nothing and no one, let alone a woman, could stay in the way of that purpose.

The purpose was the founding of Rome. Or rather, in Aeneas's case, the inauguration of propitious circumstances that led to the founding of Rome. It was his misfortune that no chronicler was present to record the glorious deeds. To be sure, no chronicler will be present for a thousand years, till the waning days of the Roman Republic, when myth became history, with history obligingly adjusting to myth. We all know how congenital to the human race is the faculty for myth. This faculty snatches any episodes, however fantastical as conveyed through the oral tradition, in the lives of those mystifying beings who stood apart from the rest. This faculty then weaves a legend out of these incidents, to which it attaches with a passionate faith, whereupon the legend becomes the champion's indisputable passport to immortality. Long live Aeneas. On this view, it was perhaps his fortune that no chronicler was present to record his deeds.

Real history began when Aeneas's descendent Gaius Julius Caesar saved Rome by turning it into a monocracy administered by one man—himself. And what a man he was—more god than man—which even his contemporaries recognized by proclaiming him "divine Caesar" after they murdered him. Well, he *was* divine, having sprung from *gens Julia,* the Julian line, the most exalted and ancient aristocratic family of Rome, claiming their origin directly from Aeneas's son Julius-Ascanius-Euryleon—and thus from Venus herself—reason "Julius" was preferred to other monikers.

Caesar's grand-nephew Octavian, known to history as Augustus, whom Caesar adopted and who thereafter became the first Roman Emperor in everything but name, was careful to maintain the divine origin. A sculpture of him, called Augustus of Prima Porta, because discovered in the Villa Prima Porta that belonged to his wife Livia, was reproduced over and over during his reign and exhibited throughout the empire for the benefit of Augustus's subjects. These subjects, in the absence of various communication devices with which our own age is blessed (or damned, depending on whom one talks to), were grateful to have a sculptural idea of what their emperor looked like, rejoicing in his divinely perennial youthfulness. The sculpture shows him as a determined young commander ready to lead his troops to battle, even if barefoot. Yet, cut in marble, he is a rather unstable young commander for all his determination, because marble is heavy and needs structural support. This is where the little Cupid comes in, riding a dolphin at Augustus's

right knee. The Cupid *is* the structural support, but he is also Venus's son. Venus came from the sea—hence the dolphin. The Julian line came from Venus—hence Cupid, the dear little cousin aeons of legendary centuries removed. No one questioned the iconography, ever ready to bow to imperial claims of divinity.

Perhaps it was the love of the sea, whence his Olympian progenitress had come, that made Augustus fall in love with Capri, where one sees the sea from every point. Perhaps that was the reason for his trading with Naples the much larger island of Ischia, which was his personal property, but where one *does not* see the sea from every point, for the tiny island of Capri which belonged to Naples. On Capri he gave full reign to his favorite hobby—building.

He had already begun to engage this passion in Rome, which, from an architectural point of view, was a sorry affair when he inherited it. The barely-evolved Romans of the early Republic were a bleak lot, who prided themselves on their austere virtues, frugal life, and military valor, and were scornful of what they considered immoral tastes and luxurious ease of their neighbors in Italy, the Etruscans and the Greeks. In the fullness of time, possessed of immorality of their own, they will learn to appreciate and cherish luxurious—nay—decadent ease, but that lay in the future. In the meantime, austere virtues, frugal life, and military valor was all this artless and doggedly resolute race had. Self-importantly they flaunted what they had.

This flaunting included neglecting their city. While their military camps and the colonial towns that resulted from them were laid out on regular plans, Rome itself grew in sadly indifferent patterns. It was a confused assortment of structures, often of several stories, built with the most slip-shod methods in order to accommodate its ever-increasing population. Still, one would expect the Romans of the late Republic, who did acquire certain pretention as a result of four centuries of evolution, to be desirous of beauty, but pretention is synonymous with arrogance, and arrogance is synonymous with hostility. In the years immediately preceding Augustus's own time, his countrymen were too busy slaughtering each other in endless civil wars to have any leisure, or funds, left over for the beautification of their city. Augustus, on taking the reins of power in his own hands, guaranteed the two essential conditions for the grand scale city-building: peace and prosperity. Toward the end of his life he would say that he inherited "Rome of brick," but was leaving it "Rome of marble."

And while building up his Rome of marble, he had plenty of that noble stone to spare for the little island he fell in love with. He could just as easily have said that he acquired Capri of picturesque huts strewn among its scenic hills, but he left Capri of many a glorious villa atop spectacular mountaintops—Belvedere one and all. One can only wonder what passed through his mind as he stood on one of his newly colonnaded terraces atop one of the island's peaks, watching seagulls in flight among sheer cliffs underneath his feet, loudly screeching their joy. From this dizzying vantage point he was able to look over the staggering views of Capri and the blue waves washing it from all sides, then retreating into the sea as far as the eye could distinguish. Did he think of Mark Anthony and Cleopatra, the two worthy foes whose combined fleets he had defeated in the Ionian Sea off the cost of Actium, in Greece? Did he think that the Ionian, as it had been during that encounter, agitated by battle and colored with blood, looked very different compared to the serene and placid Tyrrhenian Sea he was staring at now? Would Rome indeed witness years of peace after years of war and civil strife? Would it be becalmed after the storms? Did Augustus realize that after 500 years of the Roman Republic, he was inaugurating the new age, that of the Empire, destined to survive another 500 years in the

West, and still another millennium in the East, and fated forever to draw men to its glory?

We shall never know. But we do know that he loved Capri, cherished its traditions and its inhabitants. He even participated in parties organized by the island's youth, and promoted the early Greek institution of *ephebeia,* meant to build the youth into responsible citizens and train them into valiant soldiers.

Yet Augustus never made Capri his home. The senators back in Rome, lulled by him into the delusion of having some influence in the affairs of state, needed him nearby to keep up the delusion. With his successor, Tiberius, there were no longer any pretences. He was a full-fledged emperor, with absolute powers, and no regard for the Senate. He made Capri his permanent home, and a *de facto* capital of the Empire, for the capital is where the Emperor is. And this Emperor loved this tiny piece of land no less than Augustus did. Most of the surviving ruins today are from the age of Tiberius, for he continued Augustus's building program and may have built no less than twelve villas on the island. He also built stunning nymphaea in some of Capri's iridescent hidden grottos, and earned for himself, on account of these lovely fantasies in marble, a rather unfortunate reputation. Nymphaea are architectural fountain designs dedicated to Nereids, the water nymphs who controlled rivers, lakes, fountains, and of course grottos. Today, the Trevi Fountain in Rome could be called a nymphaeum. Imagine the Trevi in an enclosed beautiful cavern accessible only by a boat sliding softly through a narrow rocky waterway, the sudden sound of a cascading fountain striking one's ear before the glorious apparition of Neptune and his tritons reining in their horses met the eye? One can only try to visualize these magnificent designs in translucent marble washed over by sparkling sprays. Yet in the popular imagination, fed by sulking senators back in Rome who took exception to the emperor's antipathy for them, these nymphaea were the bedrocks of infamy and perversion. Accurate or not, the salacious rumors found their way into Tacitus's commentary and thus came down to us. Considering that Tacitus was born a century after Tiberius, had no direct proof, and filled his history with hearsay, we shall never know the truth. Just as well. As a good friend once said, why spoil a good story with the truth. It certainly did not help Tiberius's reputation that his nephew Caligula was both a madman and a degenerate, with a character so depraved that it reflected back on his uncle who had named him his successor. The uncle should have known better. Then again, Tacitus may have been right, and the uncle *may* have shared the nephew's tastes, which *would* make those nymphaea stimulating in many more ways than just aesthetic. It would also explain why the uncle named the nephew his successor.

After the death of Tiberius, Roman aristocracy lost interest in the island. With time, the marble fantasies were gone, with only wistful wrecks remaining of Neptune and his tritons in the transparent coolness of the shaded pools, the stunning Blue Grotto not least of them. Nature had asserted its rights by reclaiming these pools and returning them to their original pristine beauty. The abandoned villas overgrew with spontaneous vegetation, and over the. centuries, Ilex woods, the most extensive woods on Capri, replaced Corinthian porticos. This whole enchanted oasis in the sea, like its grottos, returned to nature and was not heard of until the 18th century, when the newly enlightened Europe came here in the hope of rediscovering between its jagged rocks the classical world of Augustus and Tiberius. Capri's popularity soared again, with the British and the French competing for its possession in the 19th century.

The island actually consists of two rocky massifs separated by a depression. One contains the village of Capri, and the other the village of Anacapri. As the names fortuitously imply, the inhabitants of either village would rather the other dropped to the sea. Ironically, in keeping with this tradition, two writers, each remarkable in his own way, and each the reverse of the other in birth, upbringing, attitudes and politics, inhabited these two villages in the early 20th century.

One was Maxim Gorky, a Russian revolutionary writer, who in the seven years he spent in the village of Capri turned it into a visiting Mecca for a heady brew of Marxist theoreticians/writers and Russian cultural figures. One such figure was Vladimir Ilyich Ulyanov, known to posterity as Lenin, the leader of the Russian Communist Revolution, who also came and didn't like the brew; too tolerant for his taste. But then Gorky, for all his revolutionary zeal, did not like the brew he saw in Lenin's new Russia.

It is the other writer, however, that the island loves and remembers. Axel Munthe, a Swedish doctor-author, built his Villa San Michele in Anacapri at the end of the 19th century and lived there most of the time till the Second World War. Unsurprisingly, his guest list differed significantly from that of Gorky's. While Gorky's list was mainly dissident, Munthe's included the Swedish royal family as regular guests, along with the *crème de la crème* of British aristocracy. And while Gorky's people quarreled over political and religious differences, Munthe's congenial guests, quietly and uniformly certain of their superiority, loved to meander among the antiquities that filled their host's elegant mansion and its stunning gardens. They must also have loved to linger on the breezy terrace that still giddily overhangs the sea, and to keep company with a large sphinx of red granite who sits on the edge of the terrace, eternally staring at the limitless panorama. As maybe Augustus stared at it two millennia back.

Armed with our captain's powerful binoculars, we nostalgically watched the sphinx diminish in size, then disappear altogether, as our ancient vessel sailed away from the Isle of Dreams toward the Isle of Sirens. Our destination was Lipari, but the looming abode of the chilling Sirens could not be bypassed, and all was disquiet. They were much worse than Circe, for it was possible to soften Circe as it turned out, but not the Sirens, who baited men with their irresistible songs and then devoured them whole. It was all well and good for Odysseus, who wished to hear them sing, to tie himself to the mast and wax his crew's ears shut so they might not hear his mad commands to moor. There weren't possibly enough masts to accommodate all of us, and in the age of electricity beeswax was in short supply. It was fortunate someone remembered that Jason, who travelled this route long before Odysseus in search of the Golden Fleece, had Orpheus on his ship, who, the moment he heard the Sirens, drew out his lyre and sang songs so beautiful that they drowned out the Sirens' bewitching strains. Surely

Odysseus must have known of Jason's experience and should have kept an able musician around. Or several. As we did. A small band with a big band spirit was presently heard, and dancing began on deck, under the stars, with endless, bird-like sails slowly billowing in a soft wind against the dark, star studded, sky. Sirens had no chance.

▼

Lipari is the largest island in the Aeolian archipelago, with a tempestuous history of Greek, Roman, Byzantine, Turkish,  Norman and Spanish occupation that makes it a veritable treasure cove for a history buff. And should a visitor doubt this fact, they have their archeological museum with its Menander masks to prove it. It is certainly one of the most interesting in Europe. As every Liparian, justifiably proud of his museum, knows, Menander, who lived in Greece at the end of the 4th century B.C., developed the New Comedy, or what we would call today the comedy of manners, the subtle observation of everyday human behavior, as opposed to the Old Comedy (by Aristophanes, for instance) that disguised political satire among sexual and scatological vulgarities. The New Comedy was sophisticated. The New Comedy influenced Shakespeare.

What better claim to fame can the New Comedy possibly have!

The New Comedy aside, however, shopping wasn't anything to disdain either, particularly considering that the beautiful Sicilian pottery was to be had for half its price in Sicily. And then there was pumice stone of Lipari's volcanic fame. Medieval monks knew of its wonderful qualities when it came to smoothing down vellum in preparation for copying ancient manuscripts, but why half the ship should have bought suitcases-full of the stuff was anybody's guess. Those who decided they had seen enough museums and would rather forgo manuscript-copying, went to wallow in the sulphurous, and presumably therapeutic, mud-flows of the near-by Vulcano Island where Vulcan, the God of Fire, keeps his forges.

Wallowing in mud done and over with, with its figurehead turned toward Sicily, the dreadful challenge facing our noble clipper was:

Here Scylla bellows from her dire abodes,
Tremendous pest, abhorr'd by men and gods!...
Twelve feet, deform'd and foul, the fiend dispreads
Six horrid necks she rears, and six terrific heads...
Beneath, Charybdis holds her boisterous reign
'Midst roaring whirlpools, and absorbs the main...

Calypso, still another demigoddess who enjoyed Odysseus's aptitude, instructed her swain before he left her that in going near Scylla and Charybdis he must be prepared to lose at least six of his crew. Now we had to face the same challenge; there was no choice. Six among us were to be forfeited to Scylla's six insatiable heads if the rest were to stay alive. The advertising brochure prior to the trip mentioned none of it.

> Ah, shun the horrid gulf! By Scylla fly
> 'Tis better six to lose, than all to die.
>
> (Homer's *Odyssey.* Book XII.
> Trans. Alexander Pope)

That night we sacrificed to Bacchus and begged protection. Here was the opportunity for us, his modern worshippers, to expose ourselves, for the good of mankind, to the ecstasy of the damned. It is doubtful that this deity, in all his life of divine debauchery, ever received a more splendid offering. The god of wine and merriment sent us sweet, inebriated dreams, in which all fears were drowned, and if six from our midst were missing the following morning, no one noticed. The huge, black, smoking cone of Mount Etna was before our eyes.

▼

Sicily was called Trinacria by the ancients because of its triangular shape. The dreaded one-eyed Cyclops Polyphemus, Neptune's gluttonous progeny, made it his home. Could the ancients have mistaken his eye for the central crater that swallows the impertinent and the curious who dare approach it, as Polyphemus had done with Odysseus's companions? Whatever the case may be, when an excursion was proposed to the top of the crater, it was politely declined by one and all. It was enough to have lost six of our group to Scylla and Charybdis—couldn't be helped—but to venture, voluntarily, into the very trap of Polyphemus's volcano would be unconscionable.

Meanwhile, there were other dangers to avoid, of which the soul of Teiresias, the blind Theban prophet of Oedipus's fame, warned Odysseus when our hero visited Hades. A delightful little yarn is told about this Teiresias who, as a young man, on walking through a forest, allegedly saw two snakes copulating. His sense of reptile propriety deeply offended, the prude forced the slithering creatures apart with a walking stick, upon which action he was turned into a woman by the magic of the vindictive reptiles. It was years before he saw another two snakes busying themselves in a similar fashion—how lucky can one get—that he was able to turn back into a male by separating them again. (Moral: anyone who wishes a sex change needs to go looking for copulating snakes rather than rely on Singapore surgeons; cheaper too). Now it came to be that Zeus and Hera, up on Mount Olympus, engaged in a heated argument whether it was men or women who enjoyed sex more fully. Zeus maintained it was women, Hera cast with the male lot. Inconclusiveness of the dispute was beginning to frustrate them both when they hit on the brilliant idea of asking Teireisias. He had been both a woman and a man, and he would 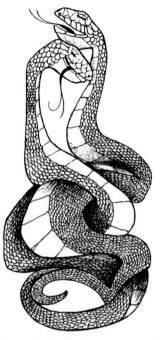 surely know. Duly summoned and queried, he pronounced women to be recipients of superior pleasure. Evidently Teireisias had better luck with his male partners than Hera did. Zeus, too smug in his righteousness to perceive the subtle subterfuge, endowed Teireisias with a gift of prophesy; Hera, vengeful in envy and defeat, struck him blind.

But I've digressed. The great danger, of which Teireisias soul warned Odysseus, lay in harming the Sun-god's cattle and fat sheep that grazed the pastures of Trinacria. No meat was to be consumed while on the island, for fear of death. Needless to say, the moment the conqueror of Troy fell asleep, his hungry companions, despite due warning, slaughtered the delectable livestock and had the satisfaction of drowning shortly thereafter on a full stomach. Our merry lot, minding the admonition, stuck to sea-food; Taormina's San Domenico Palace, converted from a 15th century Dominican monastery, is a place to have it.

The next day was spent at sea under swelling sails. A strong following wind instilled pagan joy in everyone's heart. Le Grand Jeu (the Great Game), an old tradition in Husband's school, which required various forms of odd dress, undress, and cross dress, was enacted under the auspices of the Grand Master. There were passengers running around looking quite mad. I don't think anyone even noticed that the ship was circling the Heel of the Boot, but everyone must have felt it, for the  mood was changing from classical to piratical. With good reason too. Since time immemorial, there wasn't a nation around the *Mare Nostrum*, from the age of the ancient Phoenicians to our era, that didn't pirate the Adriatic. They called themselves merchant mariners, and good old Mercury, the patron of travelers and traders, did not care to distinguish and patronized them all. The pirate's dress-up fete was now in order, and everyone obliged with a vengeance. The upside-down toilet plunger that replaced one passenger's leg would have found approval with Robert

Louis Stevenson. We thus arrived at Dubrovnik, on the Southern-most tip of Croatia, fully prepared to take by storm its redoubtable fortifications. We soon changed our minds.

▼

The fortified walls of Dubrovnik (where *Game of Thrones* was filmed, in addition to other locations) are the best preserved defense structure in Europe. They are also an arduous climb, which is why one quickly decided against piracy. Too onerous. A costume party was all well and good, but in reality buccaneering must have been an insufferable business. Much better to proceed slowly, having taken a civilized morning bath with the consequent application of deodorants to protect one from unwelcome perspiration (or hgat least its consequences), and a cool bottle of water to quench one's thirst on the way up. Frequent stops and peeks at the sun-backed red roofs as they emerge between the battlements are also recommended. It appears a number of famous literary people did the climbing and the peeking along those walls, and they all had something to say on the subject; they wouldn't be literary if they didn't. George Bernard Shaw called Dubrovnik heaven on earth, and Lord Byron pronounced it the pearl of the Adriatic. We don't know what Agatha Christie said, but she must have said something, having spent her second honeymoon here, with a husband fifteen years younger than herself. Perhaps it was too intimate for print. As to Lord Byron, it is a good thing he limited himself to pronouncements and refrained from scratching his name on the walls, as he did at the Parthenon.

201

And to think that he, the name-scratcher, had the conceit to hound Lord Elgin for vandalism, when Lord Elgin *saved* the Parthenon marbles from certain destruction, spent the greater part of his personal fortune doing so, and died in Paris in reduced circumstances. The Elgin Marbles became the foundation and the corner stone of the incomparable British Museum. Lord Byron, if he has any posthumous conscience, ought to be turning in his grave.

There was still another man of letters Dubrovnik may boast of. Richard the Lionhearted, king of England—man of letters and of swords—a crusader and a poet—who was shipwrecked on the shores of Ragusa, as Dubrovnik was then called, and built a basilica there to thank God for his deliverance. No doubt he recited some self-made verses appropriate for the occasion, in rhythm with ground digging, but none survived. Nor has the basilica survived, destroyed in an earthquake five hundred years later. Thus nothing but memory remains of King Richard in Ragusa. Yet in the unlikely event that some Ragusians may at times feel melancholy on this account, and what with misery liking company, the best possible company for the occasion is readily available to them. When Richard felt that his time on earth was drawing to a close, he directed that his body be divvied up after death, with his brain sent to Poitou, his heart to Normandy, and his embalmed corpse reverently interred in Fontevraud Abbey, Anjou, at the feet of his father, the great Henry II (with whom Richard quarreled incessantly during Henry's lifetime)—leaving not even a pinky toe for England. Surely the Ragusians could not find better company in their bemoaning the lack of Richard's remains.

But by far the most illustrious man of letters connected with Dubrovnik/Ragusa, although he never visited it, is without question the immortal Shakespeare, who set his *Twelfth Night* in Illyria, where the most important city state during the Bard's own time was the great maritime Republic of Ragusa, although he may easily not have known it, since his geography was as nebulous as that of Homer. Shakespeare seemed to think that all foreign places were sea ports, such as Milan in *Tempest,* Vienna in *Measure for Measure* (where everyone has Italian names), or Bohemia in *The Winter's Tale* (where everyone has Greek names). Most names in *Twelfth Night* are Italian, but that must have been a lucky guess, since Ragusa *was* practically Italian after centuries of Venetian domination.

Independently of Shakespeare's familiarity with it, or the lack thereof, so famous, rich and powerful was Ragusa, that it challenged Venice for the control of the Adriatic, and it was Ragusa that made Illyria famous at the time. If anyone *must* have shipwrecked, had a case of mistaken identity, and fallen in love with all the wrong people in any place in Illyria, it *had to be* in Ragusa. Additionally, the ship that so fortunately crashed on that obliging shore must have been an *argosy* ship, which Shakespeare also used in other plays. It was a merchant ship whose name derived from the Italian *ragusea*, which meant a ship from Ragusa. I picked up this invaluable piece of information by eavesdropping, up on Ragusa's fortifications, on a tour group whose guide appeared exceedingly well-informed.

There were another couple of island stops before the end of our Odyssey, where life from primordial times was still led according to primordial ways, but despite these islands' undeniable charm, or perhaps because of it, the nostalgic foreboding of this fascinating voyage's finale had cast an aura of evocative melancholy over us—the self-appointed ancient mariners—the melancholy that Odysseus surely did not feel when he finally approached his Ithaca that contained his tapestry-weaving Penelope. But then again, it took us ten days what had taken him ten years.

When upon final disembarkation water taxis took us farther and farther away from the ship, we kept craning our necks in a wistful attempt to catch the last glimpse of the five stately masts. I can safely vouch for all that in this moment everyone felt rather like a dispossessed Cinderella whose carriage was quickly turning into a pumpkin. And the pumpkin, alas, was Venice.

Other Alondra Press Books

Fiction:

Rio San Pedro, by Henry Hollenbaugh
The author's memoirs of his life as a crocodile hunter in Central America in the 1950s. Jonathan Galassi, of Farrar, Straus & Giroux says, "There is a wonderful sense of presence in this novel."

The Wind Thief, by Martha Engber
A haunting tale of the ultimate triumph of love between Ajay, the thief from Mumbai, and Madina, a strangely obsessed desert prostitute. A highly acclaimed and successful first fiction novel by Martha Engber.

The Canyon Chronicles, Volumes I and II
by K. Gray Jones
A historical novel of Utah and the conflicts between Mormons and Gentiles during the epoch from the mid 1840's to the early part of the 20th century. A masterpiece of action, drama, and unvarnished views of the Mormon church in its beginnings.

Nessus The Centaur, by Henry Hollenbaugh
A modern retelling of the ancient myth of Hercules, Dejanira and Nessus the Centaur, in which Hercules is the brutal, surly villain, and Nessus, usually dealt with as a cunning, deceitful rascal, is the tragic hero.

The Other face of Murder, by Gil Porat
An outstanding first novel by a doctor-writer, dealing with a mysterious murder among friends.

A Better Place, by Mike Flax
An engrossing novel of rebellion and the struggle for freedom, with a setting in slaveholding Louisiana and Texas, soon to be produced as a film.

Nonfiction:
Island Journeys, by Patti. M. Marxsen
Take a lyrical journey with this author across time and across seven islands with a common thread of French history

Fate, Coincidence, and the Outcome of Horse Races,
by Armando Benitez.
The author demonstrates how coincidences can be used to pick winning horses, and the wisdom in observing certain superstitious practices in order to be more successful at the track.

Common Sense Versus Wisdom, A guide to emotional control and rational thinking
by Bem P. Allen
A widely known and respected psychologist shows us how to lead a better life by recognizing and controlling our emotions.

Framing The World; Photography, Propaganda, and the Media, by Hans Durrer. Hans Durrer points out, in many entertaining stories and ways, how the media uses photography to manipulate our thoughts and opinions. Presently available only in Amazon's Kindle.

The Street Where They Lived, by Richard O'Mara
Autobiographical essays by a gifted writer, chronicling the years of his childhood and youth in Philadelphia during the years of the Great Depression.

Rhyme of the Fall of Berlin, by Henry Hollenbaugh
A mock-epic rhyming poem, in a parody of the great epic poems of antiquity and modern times. Over 4,000 lines, in eight-line stanzas.

My Eden Home, by A.R. Welm
A collection of poems launching a young artist's career. Welm's poems are frequently based on allegorical themes from ancient history and Greek mythology, with captivating illustrations by the author herself.

The Roots and Origins of Fortune and Misfortune, by Armando Benitez
The author expands the themes initiated in *Coincidence and the Outcome of Horse Races,* reinforcing his view on the logic of superstition.

Alondra Press, LLC
www.alondrapress.com